Praise for *30 DAYS TO A NEW YOU*

Just when I thought I was as fulfilled as a woman could be, astutely in touch with my inner voice, I got a jolt from **30 Days to a New You***, saying, "Wake up. You have some work to do!" My life transformed as if a lightning bolt had hit my soul and commanded, "Get beyond your story, woman. You have a Big Picture to live!" What a spiritually and psychologically deep and empowering book! I absolutely cherish Monica Magnetti.*

—Cleone Lyvonne, M.S.E.
Writer, Editor, Cover Designer

30 Days to a New You *gives you all the tools and action steps you need to change your life. I've seen Monica's powerful coaching strategies produce results quickly. This book gets right to the point and helps you get what you really want out of life.*

—Sam Beckford
Entrepreneur, Author, Coach
Co-author of *The Small Business Millionaire*

With **30 Days to a New You***, Monica Magnetti offers us again a decisive wake-up call, with a prod and a hug, to say Yes! to pushing our limits, to asking the Big Questions, to taking ownership of our lives.* **30 Days** *reminds us that there is power and magic in defining who we truly are through being present in each blessed moment —beyond judgment, beyond right and wrong —for 30 days and for the rest of our lives! I have experienced a deeper birth of purpose with Monica's new book, as I guide and witness my daily-expanding world of wonder: my full life!*

—Lynn Thompson
Radio Host & Producer, Living On Purpose

30
DAYS TO A NEW YOU

Get What You Want

Through Authentic Change

By Life & Business Coach
Monica Magnetti, BFA/CPCC

Robert D. Reed Publishers • Bandon, OR

Editor: Marj Hanhe
Cover Design: Thomas Creative Solutions
Photos of Monica: Urban Pictures
Book Design: Mait Ainsaar, BICN Marketing & Design

ISBN-13: 978-1-934759-07-3
ISBN- 10: 1-934759-07-4
Library of Congress Control Number: 2008921142

Publisher: Robert D. Reed Publishers
P.O. Box 1992, Bandon, OR 97411
Tel: 541-347-9882
Fax: 541-347-9883
E-mail: 4bobreed@msn.com
Web: www.rdrpublishers.com

Manufactured and printed in the United States of America

To my parents, Enrico and Dory

TABLE OF CONTENTS

30
THANK-YOU'S
AND THEN SOME

Writing books is my passion, and I can profoundly experience my life while I am writing because many people stand by me. The idea for *30 Days to a New You* came more than a year ago, in October 2006, after I returned from a magical trip to Vietnam. However, my two other books had to be written first for me to find my true and radical voice to write *30 Days*.

Every time I talked to people in the publishing world about this book, which was still in a shell in my brain, they would be so taken by my aliveness that they would tell me to go ahead and start writing it—contrary to their better judgment, which was that I should promote my two brand-new books first.

I have many people to thank and acknowledge for the new "me" that I become every time I write a new book. First, in the true spirit of this book, I would like to thank and acknowledge myself for walking my talk and for living the life of my dreams now. I have surrounded myself with incredible people who are precious to me; these are some of them, who went out of their way to support me so I could be the best while writing this book.

My wonderful family, who, when I get emotionally lazy, can always find one more button to push and make my life an ongoing journey of self-discovery. If it weren't for family members, who else would trigger us so deeply and make us discover the fuel for self-acceptance? I thank my mom and dad, my sisters, their partners, and their children for being in my life.

My son, Enrico, who always brings a new perspective and who, with his unexpected wisdom, flexibility, and sense of humor, brings a welcome tornado of freshness and flexibility to my life.

All the beautiful young adults in my life, who inspire me with their convictions and determination and whom I trust and respect to be the next generation running the world: Kathleen, Allegra, Sean and Ryan, Noah and Aria, Madi and Maurghen, Margherita and Mattia, a few Andreas, Bianca and Josh, Gage and Luke, Henry and Emmett, Lodovica and Alessandro, and Filippo.

My precious friends, who specifically supported me while I was writing this book: Donatella and Danny, Kim and Tony, Liz, Tana, Victoria and Anthony, Faith, Daphne, Melissa, Christine B., Wanda, Dennis, Joanne, Tricia, and Chip. Your friendship is the spark in my life that keeps me going—and my life wouldn't be so incredibly fun without you.

Steve Chandler, who has changed my life for the better. My coach, my mentor, and my friend, you are always available with an open heart and see me for all that I am.

Sam Beckford, for modeling to me how wonderful and generous a person can really be. You never stop surprising me by creating yet another new way to make this world better.

Paula Shackelton from BookBuffet and Lynn Thompson from Living on Purpose, for the enthusiasm they bring to the world and for the kindness with which they make themselves available.

I am blessed to work with the best team of people possible. With them I can do absolutely everything. I thank my editing team for individually bringing the best out of my written words: Tasha Simms, for relentlessly challenging me for the sake of text consistency; Verna Wilder, for knowing who to recommend; Julie H. Fergusson of Beacon Literary Services, for her outstanding consulting; Jennifer Blue, who has been vital to my professional life from the beginning and to whom I am profoundly thankful for being in my life; and Katie Hogan of KT Editing Services, who has been the main support in my marketing editing, and with whom I share all my first-draft brilliant ideas.

Last and definitely not least on my editing team, Marj Hahne, for being the main editor of this book and for working with me with consistency, professionalism, and a deep sense of understanding. I thank you, Marj, for respecting my words and for so caringly finding the best way to work together for the greatest results for the book.

Rebecca Peabody and Amy Reading, for being my consultant team on practical details, with tremendous expertise and open hearts. Thank you for sharing with me the gift of your knowledge.

My creative team, whom I am crazy about and who can go the distance: Cliff Thomas and Joy Moxley from Thomas Creative Solutions, for really taking my ideas to the finish line and for listening so profoundly to my creative vision that it can come alive on the page; and Mait Ainsaar from BICN for receiving with enthusiasm and professional wisdom all my creative ideas and perfecting them for the page.

My assistants, my team for the coaching shows, Tracy, Lidia and Kate, who, during the shows, take care of all the details and make me look great!

I thank my technology team's one and only member, Sone Louangxay. Sone, where would I be without you, who fixes all my tech glitches, who makes all my artistic technology ideas a reality, and who guides me, when I am having a panic attack on the weekend, to check whether my computer is plugged in? (P.S. Sone is always right! I think he has a camera focused on all the plugs for my computer!)

I am grateful for my new publishing team, Robert Reed and Cleone Lyvonne, with whom I found a brilliant new home for my writing. From the bottom of my heart, Bob and Cleone, I thank you for being so open, so enthusiastic about *30 Days to a New You*, and for being such visionaries in your field, clear about your purpose. It is very exciting to work with people who have such integrity and dreams, and who are so much fun.

And finally, I thank my clients for trusting me with their vision and their journeys. I would be nothing without you. I am humbled in the face of your greatness and courage.

Monica Magnetti

Vancouver January 8, 2008

INTRODUCTION

Yearning for Change

We have all, at one time or another, yearned to be different, to pursue a bigger project, a new job, more money, or to follow a dream or a hunch that would bring us more fulfillment. Instead of pursuing an opportunity, sometimes we stop ourself in our tracks.

What happens? Our limiting beliefs, excuses, self-doubt, and restricted thinking make us conclude that a project is too big, an effort too immense, a dream too impossible, or a goal too unreachable. We continue our own safe existence—without stretching our boundaries or capabilities. Is there a price we pay for holding ourself back? Yes. Each time we stop short, we fail to reach our potential and the thrill of running through a finish line. We remain within our comfort zone, sacrificing excitement and passion for safety and ease.

I've said this in all my other books, and I will say it again (and again): life isn't always about staying safe and comfortable. Sometimes life is about *not* being comfortable. It's about pushing ourself out of our comfort zone in order to create change or experience the satisfaction of success. Sometimes we must take risks to experience an excitement level that we will never feel if we stay seated in our metaphorical recliner, not looking outside the box or trying new things.

The Bad News and the (Very) Good News

We all love to hold on to the myth that change is hard—almost impossible—and we love to label ourself and others as stuck. This myth provides us a lot of excuses to not live our life to the fullest. We tell ourself, *If only I could change and pursue my real goals*. Yet, instead of moving forward, we willingly trap ourselves into an unexpressed life and continuously hope that something will happen—that things will magically shift into a place of fulfillment by themselves.

Well, let me confirm the truth you already know: no one is going to come and rescue you from your stuck place and magically beam you into a perfect world in which you get to live your perfect life. If you think that's bad news, think again. The good news is this: once you surrender to the fact that no one is coming to the rescue, you can make the radical move to embrace the concept that *It's Your Life* and you are capable of rescuing yourself. And, even more good news: you get to design your life just the way you want it!

A Surprising Truth: Change Is Easy

Can you pursue any goal over the course of thirty days and change into a new you? Absolutely, and this is your chance to prove it!

Because many of us operate from the understanding that change is a difficult, long, hard process, we hold on to our old self, even when we have made tremendous effort to shift to a different place. The fact is, you can easily change. All it requires to change is the time it takes to say, "I have changed." You already have. How difficult was that?

Change is immediate, smooth, and, most important, easy. Change is natural. Think about it. Change happens even if we aren't aware of it or don't want it. In fact, we are never the same from one moment to the next. Even knowing this, most of us hold on to the limiting belief that conscious change is like an insurmountable mountain. What we fail to notice is that we are the one who purposely puts the mountain across our path or designs our path with something insurmountable right in the middle.

Change Is Easy: Give It a Try (Right Now)

What would it be like to embrace the concept that *change is easy* and to let go of all your limiting beliefs, right now? I am inviting you to consciously choose to accept that change is simple. With that frame of mind, follow the guidelines of this book to find your own formula for success. Do what is actually in our nature to do: change into who you want to be by embracing and accepting that you can do anything you want to do.

Test the power of your own thoughts. Consciously shift from thinking that change is difficult to thinking that change is easy and natural. Let go of your self-imposed limitations and be open to change. Have fun and, most of all, go for it all the way! It is my wish for you that you accept yourself as the creative, resourceful, and whole person that you are. Follow the flow all the way through the next thirty exciting days to a brand-new you. No one can tell you what is appropriate for you. It's your life; design it so that it works for you.

Change: Just Do It!

30 Days to a New You: Get What You Want Through Authentic Change is a manual-style book, with work pages at the end of each chapter, of questions designed to challenge you to find the real you in the moment. As you complete the exercises, you will be pushing boundaries out of your way, clarifying your goals, and—surprise!—having a lot of fun. You will discover and design your individual steps and your formula for success as you tap into your authentic power.

Relax into success and take this book's process as far or as deeply as you want to—whether you are a corporate CEO who wants more financial recognition, an unpublished author who is looking to write a bestseller, or a parent who wants to establish a business while raising kids. We all have personal goals, dreams, and aspirations. It is by being honest with ourself about who we truly are that we can make our goals and dreams our reality.

Stick to It!

30 Days to a New You is a radical departure from my two other books because it offers a very structured formula for personal change. I continue to teach the main coaching concepts that I've created to support my clients: *Push Your Comfort Zone, Define Your Own Steps to Success, Be Your Own Rescuer, Learn How to Be Still, Be in the Present, Identify Your Values, Work At It Every Day, Really Commit to the Everyday Discipline, Create Your Blueprint*. Yet, unlike the more relaxed formula in my other books, the formula in this book is well defined.

You must stick to the formula for it to work. Every day, you must read the chapter and complete its exercises. While you may put an individual spin on the execution of the work, it must be done *every* day—even if you are in rebellion mode. On those days, simply be fast; complete the exercises without going into too much detail. Participate as deeply or as lightly as you wish; however, "stick to it" every day and trust your power within to achieve results.

For you overachievers who want to do thirty days in one day: DON'T! Don't do more than one day at a time. Follow the formula and follow the sequence of the days. Procrastinating and overachieving are opposite poles of the same issue: resistance to following directions. Follow the method the way it was designed; don't skip a day or do two or three days at once. Follow directions!

It is common for us, when we start to see results or to achieve a better place in life, to get freaked out and sabotage ourself by quitting or by messing with the formula. Catch yourself before that happens to you. Embrace that part of yourself that wants to stop or rush forward, and instead keep a steady pace. I can promise you that the results will be worth any momentary discomfort.

Finding Your Heart's Deepest Desire

Our society relentlessly pushes us to operate inside the boundaries of what we know we can achieve, rather than risk braving the unfamiliar and uncharted territory of what we really want: our heart's deepest desire. Your heart's desire is, at its essence, who you really want to be as you live the life you've dreamed of living.

We have been so conditioned to focus strictly on results that we miss the point that often the true juice and passion of fulfillment is not the achieved goal, or the destination; it's the journey to discover ourself and what we are capable of when we pursue our heart's desire.

Fulfillment is about experiencing what happens when we stretch ourself beyond our limit of what we know how to do. It's what happens when we transcend self-limitations, moving instead into a new place of confidence—where we sing rather than speak, and dance rather than walk. We move forward motivated by our heart's desire rather than by pragmatic, calculated needs or formulaic goals.

Being Big is the essential foundation necessary in order to live our life with fulfillment and outside of predictable parameters. We work toward what truly matters to us, consistent with our values. Being Big means focusing on making our dreams a reality, and really pushing ourself to be the best for our own sake, not just for results.

Wake up! We are conditioned to believe that dreams are just dreams and that life is hard and unfair. This kind of thinking makes us feel guilty about desiring more for ourself and yearning for deeper connections both with ourself and with others. Don't feel guilty. Don't judge your heart's desire. Follow the clear voice that knows what you want to achieve, and experience yourself from a new perception of limitless possibilities.

From Your Desire, Find Your Goal

Often we obsess about the one thing we don't have and so easily forget about everything else we do have, or have achieved. Ask yourself what is your most important heart's desire. What kinds of feelings do you already have that you want to experience every day—feelings that would hold you Big and empower you in everything you do? Who do you want to be in order to live a fulfilled and purposeful life? Allow yourself to hear your own inner voice respond and acknowledge your passion. This process will help you discover who you really are and who you can become.

Choosing goals comes next. This is the process of establishing what you need to do to actualize your heart's desire. Whether your goal is practical—you'd like to make more money or get married—or more intangible, such as finding balance in your life, make sure that you are holding on to the Big Picture of your heart's desire and that you truly yearn to achieve it.

*30 Days to a New You i*s designed to help you identify your true heart's desire and live your life intentionally aligned with it by guiding you to define intermediate, action-based goals that support the fulfillment of that desire. 30 Days to a New You means just that! You decide who you want to be and in thirty days you can be it.

Be in Charge of Your Life and Your Circumstances

Make sure your goals are about you accomplishing and taking charge of your circumstances, not about other people doing things to make you happy. For example, if you want a more fulfilling job, make sure your goal isn't about your boss offering you a better job. Instead, make it about you creating a better job or an opening for new offers to come in. You can't create the goal that someone will ask you to marry him or her; you can, however, create the goal to open yourself to the ideal person so that he or she may come into your life. Always make it about you.

Take full charge of your life right now by defining and declaring clear intentions that can create the optimal circumstances in your life such that you get what is important to you. Be open; listen to your heart about what you deeply want. Discover what it is that would complete you, satisfy you, and fulfill you in a deep and profound way. Don't be afraid; shoot for the stars and then trust. Trust that by listening to your heart's voice you are connecting with yourself at a deep level and manifesting what you truly desire.

The Power of Your Own Thinking

Believe in the power of your thinking and acknowledge that it may have actually created your current and past problems. You might want to blame your mother, father, boss, partner, and/or life's circumstances; however, your problems may simply have been caused by you and negative thinking—resignation, cynicism, self-doubt—that has held you back until now.

Though we like to blame our failures on everyone and everything else, including the weather, we are truly responsible for our mindset and the results we have obtained. Our thinking determines our choices, our actions, and ultimately our experience of life. It is a major step to accept that your thinking plays a major role in your success. Recognizing your limiting thoughts, stopping them, and shifting your perspective toward an acceptance of who you are and what you can do, will contribute substantially to your success.

You don't have to be in a good mood all the time. You can, though, choose to be an optimist all the time; you simply have to be conscious of what you are doing to yourself with your thoughts and then decide what you want to do about it. Your life is already perfect; the missing link is just your accepting that fact. Remarkable changes can easily happen, simply by redirecting your thoughts and allowing yourself to revise your beliefs about yourself and what you can do. When you are willing to go deeper into your understanding of yourself and to let go of rigid boundaries and the limitations you have used to define yourself, you get to discover a new person with infinite power. And when you shift the focus from just the results to the person you are becoming as you journey toward your goals, you discover that you can accomplish anything with ease and flow.

 30 Days to a New You will help you realize that your thoughts have power and that quick change is not only possible, it's easy.

Uncover the New You

30 Days to a New You is designed to support the natural flow of change, to create for you a deeper connection with your real self. This work will reconnect you with and bind you to your vision and purpose. From this place of full self-acceptance, you will be able to move forward in the direction you desire, achieving goals and completing projects from a place of authentic power—from the new you, the real you, the fulfilled you.

B4 U BEGIN

This book is designed to help you achieve tremendous results, and the best way for you to optimize those results is to complete the work-page exercises in the way that is most effective for you. If you do not enjoy writing things out by hand, you can download the Microsoft® Word file containing the 30 Days Workshop questions, and you will be able to do your work electronically instead. To download this file, simply go to www.lunacoaching.com and register to receive the file by following the directions provided on the site's homepage.

When deciding which method to use, consider what will enable you to better connect with the exercise. If the movement and personal look of your handwriting allows you to express yourself more freely, then writing on the book's work pages may be your better option. If the efficiency and ease of technology frees you up, then using the file may be the way to go.

There is no fee required to download the file, so you can try both methods! I am making this copyrighted material available to you at no charge because I want your process of self-discovery to be as authentic and enjoyable as possible. I also want you to have a template of the work pages so that you can complete the thirty-day process as often as you like, every month or with every new project, as you continue your journey of self-fulfillment. Self-realization and discovery are not one-time events; they are ongoing. Therefore, repeating these exercises over time can be very enlightening, especially as life circumstances change—and as you change.

Also, regularly check my website under "30 Days to a New You," as every month, or even more often, I will post powerful questions and creative tools only for the readers of 30 Days to a New You, so that you will stay connected to the work and to the best that you are. This is the book that keeps on giving; stay linked: Who knows where we are taking the journey?

Best wishes as you launch into the next step of your journey—the thirty days that will lead you toward creating the new you!

Day 1

Your Heart's Desire:
Design the Big Picture of Your Life

Living life following your heart's desire is about letting go of all preconceived ideas and rules and intentionally designing a life that excites you and gives you passion. It's living a life motivated by your wants rather than your shoulds. It is consciously taking charge so that you become the powerful maker of your own happiness.

This work is not for the faint of heart. This work is for bold, motivated people ready to embrace themselves with passionate abandon and dream and think Big. Your heart's desire is not called the Big Picture for nothing. This is the place to ask the Big Questions, to delve into your Big Vision and make your Big Dreams become your current reality.

If you depend on external circumstances or other people to make you happy, surrender right now to a lifetime of misery! If the weather needs to change for you to be happy, if you need to win the lottery to be happy, if you need your kids to do better in school or your spouse to listen for you to be happy, you are in trouble. If this is true for you, at least be conscious of it, embrace it intentionally, and surrender to living a miserable life.

On the other hand, if you see the possibility that you are the powerful maker of your own happiness, that you hold the key to your very own fulfilled life, then declare yourself ready to change your life right now and courageously step into your own infinite power.

What makes you tick? What fills you completely and passionately? When are you most alive? What would it be like to let go of the self-imposed chains that hold you down and to sweep yourself off your feet designing the best life ever? What would it be like to let go of all limitations and trust that there is more to life than you could ever imagine?

Stop Living Your Life in Emergency Mode

We all have been in a place, and some of us still are, where much of what we do is to take care of emergencies. We go from one crisis to another and concentrate only on survival, looking for ways to avoid or minimize loss, trying to catch our breath before another disaster calls our attention. We reserve our real life for when the kids will be older, our house will be paid for, and nobody we know is sick. We catapult ourself toward a utopia-like future in which life is, suddenly, smooth and problem-free.

Wake up. If your life is lived in survival and emergency mode, chances are the future will simply be a continuation of that. Let go of hoping that things will suddenly shift to a much better place on their own. Your habit of living life in reaction to calamities rather than from conscious choice guarantees things will never change. We confuse our heart's desire with having materialistic things and having circumstances and people around us under our control. We assign a tremendous amount of power to acquisitions, other people, and outside circumstances to fulfill us; and we neglect to see that the true essence of our happiness comes from our own capacity to make ourself happy. We can actually live an intentional life and consciously embrace our own infinite power to make ourself happy, to get what we want, to create the life we choose.

Live a Life of Intention: Choose Who You Want to Be

Shift into thinking that fulfillment is not something you can buy or own; it is something you can be. You can be fulfilled right now. You can reshape your entire life to be and feel exactly as you want. Let it spark you! You know that feeling of bubbling inside with excitement that inspires you to move forward. You can reprogram yourself to get what you want as long as you are prepared to clarify and design exactly what you desire for your life and how you want to feel in every precious second of your magnificent existence. Most important, you are willing to be who you need to be to get that for yourself. Every second that you breathe, every second that you live, is fundamentally sacred. You have been entrusted with this valuable life: live it with intention, live it with purpose, by following your heart's desire and believing in your ability to achieve it. When all your chains are broken, you are left with yourself and your own limitless capacity to make everything work for you. It's your life. Design it so that it fulfills you.

Honor your values, honor your good qualities, honor your weak qualities, honor the true you, in the moment—not the person you think you should be or the person you have held back from embracing in his or her full Bigness. Imagine the possibilities beyond your self-imposed limitations and reclaim the power to make yourself happy.

The Big Picture

The Big Picture. What is it? The Big Picture is your heart's deepest desire, and it transcends any practical or tangible goal. Does this concept seem a bit too immeasurable? Take a deep breath... and give it a chance. The tangible goals—the Small Picture—will be addressed in the next chapter, so let yourself be swept away now by the vision of how it would feel to live your ideal life.

The Big Picture is your fulfillment—consciously designing your dream life and living the feelings you want to experience every day. It is your ultimate vision of who you want to be in every moment of your life. When you experience the feelings your Big Picture generates in you, it affects your thinking process, opening you to greater possibilities and helping you guide yourself toward making good decisions even around simple day-to-day concerns.

Ask Yourself:
Who Do I Want to Be in Every Moment of My Life?

It's essential to envision your Big Picture with details that are important to you, because that is what will become your reality. Your Big Picture is about who you want to be, intentionally, in every moment of your life. It's about aligning your actions with your values and becoming the best you can possibly be. When you live your life this way, motivated by your heart's desire and acting in alignment with your values, you will love who you are. You will have integrity in all areas of your life: all that you think and feel inside will be what you express on the outside. You will never have to hide yourself again.

We have been so conditioned to focus on results that we miss the point: often the true zest in life comes from the journey toward the destination, not from the arrival. The most critical part of this journey is to assess your heart's true desire and to commit to living day-by-day, moment-by-moment, stretching yourself beyond the limits of what you already know and know you can do. These incremental expansions allow you to test your gut—and build your faith in it—to guide you as you pursue your deepest passions.

Ask Yourself:
What Would It Be Like to Live Life Motivated by My Heart's Desire?

Surrender to the thought that your dream life is just a step away. All you have to do is to design it. At the end of this chapter, you will get to write down your heart's desire and experience what it feels like to hold yourself Big. Take a moment now to imagine. Imagine living your life consciously, deliberately, with the commitment to consistently grow and become an authentic human being. Imagine fully embracing the journey of getting to know yourself, broadening your experience of yourself without judgment. Imagine experiencing the juice of a life lived with intention, fully claiming ownership of who you are becoming, and honoring the values you discover on your journey. Imagine becoming the person you never dared to imagine you could be.

Envision:
Be Myself Living My Own Life at My Biggest.

I am here to fully support you in defining your heart's desire and consequently taking charge of your life in a way you have not yet experienced. I have designed this chapter to support you in empowering yourself, in being powerful. Together, we will bring out your most alive and passionate self. You are creative, resourceful, and whole; and now you are in a safe and creative space where you can trust yourself to bring forward a vision of the Biggest person you can be. I am here for you, championing you, provoking and pushing you, holding you Big—even if you have trouble imagining yourself that way!

Right now, let go of the need to look good at all times. Let go of self-judgment; let go of esteeming only your gracious qualities—that is so boring! I can tell you for a fact: looking good, judging yourself, and being "nice" is not working. You are here to embrace your complexity with pride and to envision all that you can be—which means accepting your failures and your not-so-hot qualities. Your perfection lies in your human imperfections. As soon as self-judgment is out of the picture, you will embrace yourself for the extraordinary human being that you are.

Let yourself be who you can be when you come from passion and authenticity. Don't contrive yourself to be the human being you think you should be. Instead, relax and know that you can rewrite your story and reinvent yourself once you discover the real you. Embrace the radical act of living your life according to your values, with continual attention to wellness in all areas of your life. See yourself being able to accept your failures as well as your successes. Step with confidence into assessing your weaknesses from a point of strength, not self-judgment. This courageous act of revisiting your life from a self-empowered, self-discerning perspective generates a present filled with choices and a future filled with possibilities.

Ask yourself what is your most cherished dream at this point in your life? Is it to trust yourself and know that you are always at the right place at the right time? Is it to live a life in partnership with another, with harmony and mutual understanding? Is it to never have to worry about money, to have financial freedom? Is it to be healthy in all areas of your life, to wake up every morning jumping out of bed to live your life to the fullest? Is your most cherished dream to experience a sense of purpose with your life? Or is it to help others find their direction? Is your heart's desire realized in the smiles of your children when you pick them up from school? Is your most cherished dream to know that you have left a mark on this world and you will be remembered, to know that your life has had meaning?

WORKBOOK: Day 1

Date: D / M / Y

Your Heart's Desire: Defining Who You Want to Be

As you answer the following question, remember to keep the focus on yourself, not on other people and how you might want them to be. For your answers, you might consider such feelings as these: competent, self-confident, radiant, trusting, relaxed, comfortable in my own knowledge and capacities.

What feelings do you yearn to experience in your day-to-day life, in your work life, and in your relationships with yourself and others?

Day-to-Day Life   Work Life   Relationships with Self & Others

Imagine you have a magic wand that you can wave to instantly become the exact kind of person you want to be. Close your eyes for a moment and breathe into the feelings you identified above. Let your imagination soar as you wave your magic wand and describe exactly who your ideal self is.

How would you act if you were your ideal self? In what ways would you act differently in these three areas of your life if you were your ideal self right now?

Day-to-Day Life   Work Life   Relationships with Self & Others

What is the biggest unresolved issue in your life right now? If you were looking at this issue through the eyes of your ideal self, if you had his or her perspective, how would you resolve this issue?

What does your life look like with this issue out of the way? Be specific in all three areas of your life. What would your day-to-day life look like with this issue out of the way? Your work life? Who would you be in your relationships with yourself and others without this issue?

Day-to-Day Life   Work Life   Relationships with Self & Others

Breathe into your ideal self; breathe big, deep breaths into every cell of your body; and let your ideal self complete the following sentence with three distinct answers.

I am a person who stands for _____ .

Breathe this in and own it.

I am a person who stands for _____ .

Breathe this in and own it.

I am a person who stands for _____ .

Breathe this in and own it:

These are your top three values. Remember them; cherish them. You will be using them to consciously create the life you want.

Congratulations! You have now created the Big Picture of who you will be and how it will feel to live your ideal life.

Day 2

Define Your Goals:
Create Your Benchmarks

Relax! You know where you're headed. Yesterday you envisioned your Big Picture and formulated a clearer idea of how you'd like to be living your life. Now, on Day 2 of your radical transformation toward your optimal self, you will assess what practical steps you can take to create your Big Picture. In one of today's exercises, you will define your goals, and those goals will become benchmarks on your path as you walk toward your success. The Big Picture is your heart's desire. Your goals—the Small Picture—is how you will get there.

     In life, there will always be specific challenges and issues that arise: career, health, time management, dealing with loss, losing extra weight, gaining weight, making more money, children growing up, and other such matters that are unique to you and your experience. Resolving these challenges must be your priority, your goal, your Small Picture, so they will no longer be your excuses for slow, or no, progress.

For example, if you want to live your life loving your work and feeling appreciated for it, you may need to find a new job. Getting a new job, then, will become your immediate goal. If your relationship is not fulfilling, your immediate goal will be to research solutions and proactively do something about it. You will have many specific goals in your life, and the actualization of them will bring you the experience of living your Big Picture. Your goals and your Big Picture are intrinsically linked because how you achieve your goals, your Small Picture, will demonstrate who you are as a person and will give you the feeling experience of your Big Picture.

Keep Your Eyes Wide Open

A client had set her heart on exercising her power and making choices, rather than moping through life driven by circumstances. This was her Big Picture. She wanted to empower herself by doing something grandiose and totally out of character, so that she could prove to the world she was worthy of being a princess. Her goal was to marry Prince Albert of Monaco. She truly believed that the pursuit of this goal, her Small Picture, would completely fulfill her. The Prince was, after all, single. She told herself that she would stop her quest if he got married, since her bottom line, a value she didn't want to betray, was to not become involved with a married man.

In the desire to reach her goal, she addressed many issues. She focused on her health, lost a substantial amount of weight, committed to an exercise routine, discovered her ideal eating regimen, and became interested in fashion. In order to express her new expensive tastes, she got a job with a higher salary and went to France for six months to learn French. She had decided this was essential so that she could communicate with her future husband in his native language. While in Paris taking her French course, she fell in love with a man and eventually married him. She loves her life.

In the quest of her Small Picture, she learned how to push her comfort zone, use self-discipline, respect herself, and let go of the stories that were holding her back. In the pursuit of her extravagant goal, she grew to love herself and became very curious about life. She started making choices motivated by her own desires. She ended up marrying a prince—it just wasn't Prince Albert. More important, she now lives in alignment with her heart's desire, which is to experience herself coming from a place of power, accepting herself as the princess she really is, no matter what anyone else thinks.

The point of this story is to always keep the focus on yourself while pursuing your goals and realizing your heart's desire, because *your* transformation is the objective—and it will be your reward.

The reason to keep the Small Picture—your goals—aligned with the Big Picture—your heart's desire—is because, as in the story above, things may not happen the way you planned, and your goals may shift as you walk toward achieving your heart's desire.

If you focus only on results, you may be disappointed if circumstances change. When you stay focused on yourself, on the person you are becoming and the feelings you are experiencing while in pursuit of your goals, you will always have a deeper learning experience and a more accurate gauge of your progress.

Making a million dollars, or selling a million books, doesn't necessarily create the happiness that we expect it will create. If you keep the focus on yourself, however—on how you are being and feeling—during the process of making or selling millions, you will be in a place of tremendous awareness and learning.

When you keep the focus on what you are learning about yourself along the way, it will always be of value, no matter what goals you end up achieving. Focus on the process and on what you like about yourself, what you don't like about yourself, what works for you, and what doesn't work for you as you pursue your goals. This way, you will discover that the whole point is to observe your transformation. Then you will be able to make an inventory of what you want to experience again, and what you never want to experience again, in the pursuit of any future goals.

Ask Yourself:
What's in the Way of My Living My Big Picture?

Keeping your Big Picture in mind is important when setting your goals because it also connects you with the feelings you value most. Once you experience how it will feel to live life Big and completely fulfilled, it will be easier to determine what stands in the way of your getting there. Make it a priority to resolve what stands in the way of your living Big, as it will direct how you define your goals.

Working toward your goals requires you to transcend limiting boundaries and reach beyond your comfort zone, so that you can experience yourself from a place of expansion. Paraphrasing Albert Einstein, one can't resolve an issue with the same consciousness that created it.

Don't get caught up with accomplishing only your defined, practical goals; any issues that come your way will give you the opportunity to demonstrate what kind of person you would like to be. Remember, the journey is not only about the destination; it's also about broadening your experience of yourself while you are in the process of trying something new.

Be proud of your goals; life is too short to waste time judging yourself. Whether you want to make more money, lose weight, or write a book, ensure that your goals stretch your boundaries and support you in living your life from the radical place of fulfillment that comes from aligning your actions with your values.

Whatever you want that will bring you closer to your ideal life, remember that they are *your* wants and aspirations; accept them with the integrity with which you intend them. For example, many people believe that spirituality and wealth are mutually exclusive, that wanting more money is incompatible with our spiritual integrity. There is no wrong way to do this; there is only your way, which, in the world of possibilities, is a right way.

So what stands in the way of your living Big right now?

Try It Differently This Time: Create Goals That Connect You with YOU

Most of us love to shoot for the stars and set goals that aim for perfection. When we do this, our goals generally assume gigantic proportions and become a mirage, like an oasis of water and shadow in the arid desert, projected far away from us. Even though setting goals is actually an admirable exercise, which you will be doing in the chapter-end work pages, a typical, conventional structure causes us to place our goals out of reach such that they dangle like a carrot just beyond our nose. With the structure presented in this book, you will look for goals that immediately enliven you, ignite a connection within you; and you will set reasonable time frames for their attainment.

Think about your internal messaging: *When I lose thirty pounds, I will buy myself new clothes and look fabulous. When the pain in my back goes away, I will start running and be happy. When I meet the ideal partner, my life will be complete. When I get pregnant, I will feel like I have it all. When I close another sale, get another raise, or make another million, I will finally take a holiday.*

Sound familiar? Often our goals are so far away that we don't allow ourself to live life *now*. We set a goal into the distant future, and then hold our breath as we metaphorically dive underwater to pursue what we think is our ultimate desire. Our goal gets so powerfully embedded in our psyche that by the time we reach it, we have missed much of life along the way. And what's worse, we will immediately set another goal and forget to breathe for another ten years!

There are always more pounds to lose, more babies to nurture, more dates to make, more paychecks to deposit. This time, do it differently: set up each goal in alignment with your heart's desire and keep the focus on *what you are doing* to achieve your goal and on *who you are becoming* as you achieve your goal. Ask yourself what it would be like to live your life to the fullest while in the process of reaching your goals. Take a deep breath, relax, and surrender to this new vision.

Discover the Power: Assess What's Right for You—in the Moment

When my clients have big goals, I suggest to them that they break down the goals into stages and that, between the stages, they really breathe in, making time to acknowledge the life they are living now, as they work to accomplish their goals. It is helpful to delineate the stages at measurable intervals so that you can periodically gauge your success and reassess the goal. The process of breaking down your goals into smaller steps also gives you a chance to be present to the process you are in. It allows you to breathe deeply, to appreciate the journey and each small success you make—and to acknowledge yourself. Your life is not just about achieving the goals you set for yourself; it's about living a balanced life to the fullest, and in the present, as you work to realize your dreams.

When your goals are broken down into smaller chunks, they become less of a mirage or a dangling carrot, and more manageable and attainable. Remember, this is *30 Days to A New You*. As long as you are alive, you are a work in progress. Decide what you want to set up and achieve in thirty days and also what needs to happen after that. Make this process work for you. It is structured for you to succeed on multiple levels; design it so it works for you.

None of Us Are Superhuman, Including You

When we set our goals too high for ourself to reach, we subconsciously set ourself up for failure. Then we deride ourself because we are not superhuman; we believe we *should* be able to achieve the desired results. When we set up a *should*-driven goal, we invariably become disappointed with our performance because all the emphasis is on the immediate result and not on the process. For your goal-setting exercise, keep in mind the Big Picture of *who you are becoming* while you are working on your goal, in addition to *what you are doing* to reach the goal.

When setting a goal, do not pull arbitrary numbers or objectives out of your head. Instead, go deep into your body and ask yourself to consider the possibilities: *Where is the stretch for me? How do I want to feel? Is there excitement? Do I feel* alive? Then, just be. Be willing to listen to answers from within. From a place of connection with your body and your heart's desire, you will be able to assess all the possibilities, all your desires, and set your goals from a clear, empowered place.

Goals are tools you use to acquire self-knowledge as well as to move yourself forward. Make this process your process and don't judge it. Simply assess it by way of the vitality and excitement you feel within yourself. Harmonize with what you want to do, and the world will harmonize with you. Remember, if you're working too hard, your process is not working. Your life can be easy. Align the practical steps with your inner magic, your inner desire, your essence, and your Big Picture. Dream a little and listen to the answers you get from your gut. I have witnessed time and time again that gut reactions and answers are generally the most accurate.

Start Now: Live Your Life in the Present

I catch myself saying all the time to my clients, "Take a deep breath; sink into your body. How would it feel to have a life while you work toward your goal?" I ask them, "What would it feel like to actually look very professional while on the way to making your first million dollars? How would it feel to look fabulous while you're busy working at losing the pounds you want to shed?" I ask them to consider how great life would be if they could be happy while they are in the present and working toward their goals. I ask them to take a deep breath and give themselves what they wish to receive from their ideal partner rather than wait to receive it from someone they've yet to meet. I ask them to envision giving power to themselves, in the present, in order to live the life they dream of right now.

Ask Yourself:
What If Nothing Needs Fixing? (Imagine that!)

Take a deep breath and stop preparing to live the perfect life. Live your life as it is right now, because it's already perfect.

WORKBOOK: DAY 2

DATE: D / M / Y

Your Small Picture: Identifying Obstacles and Setting Goals

Here are some suggestions of areas you may want to address. Identify any others that are relevant to you, and list them below.

Keeping in mind your Big Picture, what is standing in the way of your living your best life in any of the following areas?

- Day-to-day life

- Work

- Relationships with self & others

- Health

- Education

- Personal expression

- Creativity

Assess your goals in stages and take your time; this is a work in progress! For example, if you want to lose 30 pounds or make a million dollars, break down the process of achieving your goal into measurable results and reasonable time intervals.

In 30 days, I will _____

In 60 days, I will _____

Take a deep breath and be willing to hear your inner voice. Strategize, prioritize, and allow your intention to live your Big life and come from your heart's desire.

Hear your inner voice with clarity and focus. Be present to the wonderful journey you are designing for yourself. Savor the moment. Focus on the goals that will bring you closer to fulfillment. You can have as many goals as you want to have, and you can come back to this list whenever you wish, and go a step deeper.

DAY 3

YOUR PURPOSE AND VISION: DO YOU REMEMBER WHO YOU ARE?

We all have, in the depth of our consciousness, great ideals and hopes of somehow changing the world or our surroundings with our presence. It's beautiful and noble to believe we were put on this planet, or chose to come into this world, to leave our unique mark and to make a difference. Small changes, big changes, we all hold in our heart the powerful and sincere desire to touch someone's life—maybe even our own.

Children dream big. When people ask kids what they want to be when they grow up, children have no problem expressing their desire to be an astronaut or a nurse or a doctor or a flight attendant. Children don't judge jobs. Remember when you were a child? You were curious, and you said what you felt in the moment. You had the flexibility to change your mind according to your desire, and you believed that you would be great at whatever you chose to do.

When we were children, we were intrinsically proud of who we were and had no fear in expressing who we wanted to be or what we wanted to do. As we grew older, we took on limitations as if they were real! We allowed ourself to be molded by our family and by centuries of tradition, and, as a result, we started shrinking our big vision of ourself. It's disheartening—and true. We became embarrassed of our purpose, and have made the "what we do" more important than the "who we are." We have settled for what we can get, and have made choices based on what others want for us, what is safe, and what doesn't push us too far out of our comfort zone.

Try something different? We don't want to risk it! Instead, we spend our days caught up in solving immediate crises, unconsciously abandoning who we are and what we were supposed to do, in favor of practicality and pleasing those around us. If only we could see that when we are willing to identify and connect with our purpose and vision, we become so profoundly aware and confident in our infinite power that we can take risks, simply *relaxing in the knowing* that we are on track with ourself.

Ask Yourself:
What's Keeping Me From Dreaming the Way I Used To?

We don't want to be hurt; we don't want our children to be hurt. Yet, by avoiding pain and living small and safe, we bring in the absolute opposite of what we want, and then we judge what we get. We hear it all the time: "Don't talk about your dreams or they won't come true." It's crazy thinking! How are your dreams going to become a reality if you are not willing to talk about them and create the openings in your outer world for them to come to fruition?

Do you want to keep depriving yourself of experiencing how it feels to express your dreams to your closest friends and loved ones? Don't you want to observe their reactions to your heartfelt enthusiasm? People will be touched by you and your vision if you first allow yourself to be in touch with, and touched by, your dreams and aspirations—the ones you've had since childhood.

Often, it's as if we are making a pact with life that we will stay as small as we can, passing under the radar, in exchange for comfort and safety. We even shrink in our body and forget to walk tall and strong, with the convictions of our dreams to support us. In that place of mental confinement, there is no room for purpose or vision, because purpose and vision need Bigness. They need space, creativity, messiness, unpredictability, curiosity, and infinite trust—in ourself, *in who we are and can become.*

Take a Stand: Define Your Purpose

Your purpose is about *who you are* when you are living your best life, a life based on your heart's desire. This can be who you are metaphorically or who you are in your reality. It helps to use your body, to feel in your body, when you are connecting with your purpose. Defining your purpose will further connect you with your Big Picture and your goals, and will support you in consciously living a life of choice, in which you are fully alive.

A fulfilled life is a life lived intentionally, with purpose and trust in your own vision and in the gifts you wish to share with the world. Defining your purpose will support you in finding more direction in your life and will sustain you in moments when your path is unclear or uncertain. The declaration of purpose you will create in this chapter's exercise will help you connect more easily with your inner self so that your voice overpowers the voices of others. Your purpose statement will inspire you to always trust your choices and to never allow others' opinions to chip away at your confidence.

WORKBOOK: Day 3

Date: D / M / Y

Creating Your Declaration of Purpose

Work as long as you like on your purpose statement, and keep revisiting it until you are completely satisfied. In this book, you are asked to commit to working the days chronologically; however, you can keep going back to previous days to deepen what you have already done. Relax. You will know when you have found your declaration of purpose. Trust. You may find it helpful to answer these questions to support your discovery:

- What are the gifts I can share with others?

- What wisdom can I share?

- What will I leave behind? What is my legacy?

- What difference will I make in the lives of others?

- What am I being called to give?

You will be creating a statement similar to these examples:

- *I am the photographer who, with my magical eye and my warm heart, connects mankind with nature.*

- *I am the storyteller who connects people to their inner and outer natures.*

- *I am the editor who supports people in finding their written voice so they can tell their stories.*

- *I am the lighthouse who illuminates people's paths in the dark and shows them their journey.*

- *I am the healer who helps others see their own divine potential.*

- *I am the scientist who gives comfort and hope to people in pain.*

Now it's your turn. Find a place where you will not be disturbed. Get comfortable and focus on your breathing. Deepen your breath, connect to your power center, and let go. Answer the question below when you are ready. Take your time; go slowly; enjoy the process. Let the metaphors come to you.

What is your life purpose?

I am the _____ who _____

Be willing to declare your purpose out loud and really experience how it feels in your body. Don't worry about being silly: shout it out loud; embody it; let it fill the room. Declare it at least three times.

DAY 4

CREATE AN ATMOSPHERE:
THE POWER TO CHOOSE YOUR SURROUNDINGS

We often give our power away, thinking that so many things in life are circumstantial rather than set in motion by our own consciousness. We honestly believe that fate rules our life more than we do! If we are conscious, we know we get to choose to live our life the way we want to. We get to intentionally design it, creating our ideal circumstances as our strong foundation. In one of today's exercises, you will determine what atmosphere you want to experience in your life while you pursue your heart's desire and your goals. By atmosphere, I mean the temperament of your surroundings. You get to decide if your surroundings are peaceful and serene, or hustle and bustle. It's your choice; choose the type of atmosphere that gets you the most results.

This is another place for you to be honest with yourself, to be aware of what works for you, as you identify and establish the conditions you prosper in. Do you want an atmosphere of self-trust? Do you want to design an atmosphere that creates enough tension to fuel your creativity? How does your creativity get fueled? Do you need peace and quiet? Silence? An atmosphere can be declared in practical terms—no disturbances or noises, for example—or metaphorically: you want spaciousness or trust in yourself. It's your atmosphere; you get to design it.

Be on the Lookout: Watch Your Thoughts!

In creating your atmosphere, you also want to watch your thoughts, because so often it is our thoughts that produce an atmosphere of serenity or tension within ourself. The following thought-watching process is adapted from The Work of Byron Katie (www.thework.com). When you have a thought that brings you out of the perfect reality that is your life, ask yourself, *Is this really true?* Notice who you become when you hold on to that thought, and then ask yourself, *Who would I be without this thought?* Then assess if the opposite of that thought can be as true or truer than the original thought. Notice what changes in yourself and in the general atmosphere of your surroundings.

Say you have the thought "I'm not good enough; I can't do anything right." Is that really true? Is it really possible that you never do anything right? Can you think of three things you actually do right, according to your parameters, not those of others? I'm sure you can! Then take a deep breath and ask yourself, *Who would I be without this thought?* Most of us lighten up and drop our shoulders as soon as we ask this question. Then turn it around: *Who would I be if the opposite was true: I am good enough and I do everything right?* That *can* be true! You may be doing everything right according to your values, your purpose, and your vision.

When we are mean toward ourself or have thoughts that don't support us in realizing our higher self, we set up an atmosphere of doubt and frustration in which we can't do anything right. We become self-critical to the point of destruction, and we stop the flow of life—disrupting and destroying the creative space we need in order to operate at our best. Our thought process establishes the atmosphere that will guide us to success or failure. What atmosphere do you require to be at your best? There is no right or wrong answer; this is about you, so make it work for you.

Take Charge: Define Your Own Parameters

Often we don't see how successful we are because our thought process causes us to self-assess according to parameters that are not really ours. We expect impossible outcomes or hold ourself to standards of success that are not in tune with our own values or capabilities. Consequently, we never get what we want when we measure ourself according to what other people want. Creating an atmosphere conducive to personal success requires surrendering to your unique individuality and accepting that your standards and your parameters are right for you. Relax into success; relax into your success. Your job is to make yourself happy; and when you are happy, the rest of the world simply yields to you. It's really that easy.

Repeat After Me: *Change Is Easy.*

Creating an intentional life involves becoming aware of all the ways you unconsciously abuse yourself, determining what changes you need to implement to create an atmosphere that supports your Small Picture, and then making the conscious effort to shift to a more positive place by taking action and monitoring your thoughts. If two different thoughts create two completely opposite atmospheres, one that works and one that definitely doesn't, which thought would you choose to hold on to? Change is easy as long as you are willing to believe it—as long as you are willing to embrace your own responsibility for what you have in your life and what you are willing to create.

Be Your Best Ally

Our relationship with ourself is a critical one, because few will treat us better than we treat ourself—and often we abuse ourself. In today's exercises, you will deliberately observe your thoughts and design an alliance with yourself for how you will treat yourself, regardless of the circumstances life throws your way.

What way of treating yourself will have the most value for you at this time in your life, both when things go smoothly as you proceed in the direction you have planned, and when things suddenly go sideways? For instance, you may want to be encouraging with yourself, or excited and pleased, whether or not things go according to plan. Sometimes it is precisely in the moments that do not conform to our plans that we glean the most learning.

It's great to have a plan, yet we tend to forget that there is something called *life* that can foil our perfect design! Yes, life often gets in the way because we make plans from our comfort zone and are attached to things looking a certain way. We are conditioned to think that if we don't get the exact results we expected, then our efforts have to be labeled a failure. This is unfortunate, since it is the ability to dance in the moment with life and its unforeseeable circumstances that brings flexibility, and it is the unexpected twists to our routines that bring a wealth of knowledge and experience.

Often such circumstances also bring *better* results and a lot more fulfillment—if only we would be willing to embrace ourself for the elegant, spontaneous dancer that we naturally are. We were born to think on our feet. We are equipped to shift, to change our perception to a more fluid way of thinking and get energized by circumstances that challenge us to live outside the box. That is who we naturally are.

Ask Yourself: *What Am I Thinking?*

Intentionally work on your thoughts, deciding which ones to let go of so that you can design your ideal atmosphere—one that will foster your natural place of creativity, where fluid thinking and flowing actions are effortless, appreciated, and rewarded by the conscious you.

WORKBOOK: Day 4

Determining Your Ideal Atmosphere

What qualities of atmosphere cultivate your most creative, productive, and resourceful frame of mind such that you can achieve your goals? Assess your possibilities, and always stretch yourself to find the answers that are tailored to you. String together as many possibilities as you want. The word "and" is one of the most powerful words in the English language. It is an invitation to multiply possibilities. Really find the attributes that most excite you <u>and</u> bring you alive <u>and</u> keep you centered.

For example: trust <u>and</u> serenity <u>and</u> fulfillment <u>and</u> understanding <u>and</u> cutting-myself-some-slack <u>and</u> openness <u>and</u> relaxation <u>and</u> effervescence <u>and</u> curiosity <u>and</u>...

What thoughts about yourself do you need to let go of to create that atmosphere in your life?

Watching Your Thoughts

Do this exercise with as many of your perpetual negative thoughts as you wish. Think of the thought and then answer these questions:

- Is this thought really true?

- How do I treat myself when I have this thought?

- Who would I be without this thought?

- Who would I be if the opposite was true?

Notice how much easier it is to achieve a state of well-being when you dwell in positive thoughts.

Creating an Alliance with Yourself

Reflect on your recent pursuits and answer these questions:

How do you treat yourself...

- *...when things proceed according to plan?*

- *...when things go sideways?*

What way of treating yourself would be more conducive to your happiness and fulfillment...

- *...when things proceed according to plan?*

- *...when things go sideways?*

What essential qualities are important for you to hold on to in all of life's circumstances? Choose as many as you want—ALL the ones that are important to you—and string them together with "and." You can have them all; they don't exclude each other.

For example: flexibility and light-heartedness and fun and seriousness and professionalism and goofiness and....

Day 5

Update Your Stories:
It's Time to Live Your Life, Not Theirs

There are stories that run our life. Today, we open up to the process of "updating our system" by updating our stories. I don't know how, where, or when our story-making starts. However, I've noticed, in my own personal journey and that of my clients, that we all seem to have talked ourselves into believing a series of stories about *who we are*. Most of the time, these stories stop us from moving forward in constructive ways, and they are used as subconscious excuses to play it safe. The more we go on in life, the more elaborate and detrimental these stories become, limiting us in our ability to take risks or assess if the stories are even true. When we hang on to a rigid story about ourself, we remain victimized by its "truth" because we forget that we authored it! We lose our curiosity, we lose our fascination for life, and we lose the ability to see the shades of possibility any situation might offer.

We have made and continue to make up stories about *who we are* with respect to our parents, our teachers, our friends, and our jobs—as well as with respect to ourself. Instead of creating stories that support our expansion, we create stories that hold us back, confine us, and keep us fixed in our points of view: "I was never good in math, because in second grade my teacher...blah, blah, blah..." That was forty years ago! By now, the story has been so developed, retold over and over, with all the tragic details filled in, that the storyteller actually believes it whether it is true or not.

I've challenged many of my clients on their stories based on the observable fact that their behavior didn't match their information. Once they became conscious of their limiting stories, and of their authorship of those stories, much to their surprise, they were able to easily update old information and let go of many of their timeworn stories. They could now move forward with a fresh, updated perspective of themselves and the self-awareness to identify and reject those stories when they try to re-enter their "system."

It's Time for a Clean Slate: How to Update Your System

We update our computer with new information all the time. We update programs, cellular phones, and answering systems. We have to have the latest technology, yet we are not willing to reassess *who we are* on a regular basis, or update ourself and our belief system.

"I have a fear of intimacy because..." "I don't like school because..." "I'm not good at this or that because when I was three, someone said or did this or that..." "I am not very good at relationship..." We listen to these stories in our heads, and we tell them to people at the bus stop, in the dentist's chair, in the checkout line, without recognizing how paralyzing these stories are. By unconsciously embracing such stories and perpetuating them, we are often holding on to something someone said to us, sometimes more than half a century ago, and we live life conditioned by these self-defeating thoughts and speech. We end up giving our power away to people who, most of the time, said something unintentionally; and we decided to hold on to it forever, interpreting it to mean something personal about ourself, letting it shape our belief system, when it might have meant something entirely different! You may think I'm exaggerating. I'm not. I'm challenging you to go deeper into your own stories, your own limiting self-beliefs, and observe, with a curious attitude, where you use those elaborate stories to keep yourself from playing Big.

I had a client who judged herself to be unreliable, though there was no evidence for it since she was always on time and well prepared. When I challenged her belief, she was surprised; she had never questioned it. She was told at a young age by a teacher that she was unreliable, and she took that information on as the truth and let it shape her entire life, even though she didn't remember the circumstances that prompted the comment.

I have met people who thought they couldn't take a specific university course of study because their parents had told them which subjects they excelled in and which ones they struggled with: "You are just like me: math is not your subject." Sometimes our parents set unwarranted limitations on us—passing down their stories that likely aren't even true. If we are not conscious and willing to regularly update our reality by clearing disempowering stories from our belief system, we risk setting the same limitations on our children. Instead of creating a belief system in which the sky is the limit, our society is invested in creating overly cautious, suppressed individuals unconscious of their own infinite power and capacities.

Think about your deepest heart's desire—your Big Picture—and your goals, and then ask yourself what stories have run your belief system. What stories have held you back from identifying your full potential and range of possibilities?

Cut Yourself Some Slack: You're Perfect Without Those Stories

You are perfect. If you could cut yourself some slack around your perceived imperfections, you'd see that you are human. It would be much easier to empower yourself by reframing your weaknesses as tools that can push you forward. So, you're not good in math? That's a great advantage in dealing with people who might also not be good in math. Or, you might take more classes, test it out, challenge yourself in some creative ways, and change the course of history!

Reality is perfect. What makes it *imperfect* are our thoughts about ourself and the stories we've invented, leaving no space for flexibility or the present truth. There is treasure in everything. The essence of this process is to realize that you don't have to be good at everything at all times, and at all costs. Sometimes we really are not good at math. Period. The point is to observe whether that information is a correct assessment of yourself in the present moment, or a debilitating story that might not even be true. Having a clear and correct assessment of yourself, moment by moment, is empowering—different from carrying an old judging story that just gives you another excuse to play small.

When you catch yourself being run by a story, stop. Breathe and ask yourself, *Is this who I really am in the present?* Be willing to be curious, to be interested, and, based on what you discover, to update your belief system. What if it isn't true that your mother liked your brother more? What if you aren't the inconsiderate chauvinist your first girlfriend said you were? What if it isn't true that you can't make money because you're lazy? What if you don't have a fear of intimacy? What if it's actually easy for you to move on from the disappointment of your divorce? What if disappointment turns out to be the greatest learning lesson of your life? *What if?*

WORKBOOK: Day 5

DATE: D / M / Y

Assessing Your Stories

Ask yourself what stories might be holding you back from achieving your goals and your Big Picture. Write down all the stories you believe about yourself and, for each one, ask, Does this story reflect who I truly am in this present moment? *Then write down how each story is holding you back. Be willing to listen to your authentic voice and to rewrite your limiting stories. Only you know what's true for you.*

Limiting Stories about Myself: How Is This Story Holding Me Back?:

Who would you be without your stories? If none of them were true, if you were free from all those limiting myths and beliefs about yourself, who would you be? This is another opportunity to get out of the structure of your life and really dream Big. The radical act of living an intentional life is to be aware of everything that holds you back and to rewrite it coming from an accurate assessment of who you are in the present.

Describe yourself as the person you really are. Detail what your life would look like if you were not bound by your old stories.

What is the new reality you want to design for yourself? Be specific and leave it as an open-ended story, with flexibility for ongoing reassessment.

Day 6

Become Curious:
Listen and Be Surprised Every Day

Curiosity is underrated, undervalued, and, in some of us, just about nonexistent. Not many of us are actually curious anymore. When was the last time you asked a question without knowing or assuming the answer? No, really. When we have it all figured out—our world and everyone else's— there is very little space to be curious. By falling victim to our own stories, we have lost interest in wanting to know how we *really* feel about something, or how anyone else *really* feels. How predictable!

How many times have you witnessed or participated in this scene? A loved one displays curious interest about what we think or feel in a situation, and instead of answering them honestly, we turn around and snap, "You don't know how I feel about that?" It's as if the likelihood of revisiting our opinion on something is as remote as our traveling to the moon.

In the scene above, the attitude and reply promptly and essentially kills the flow of life. When we shut that door to conversation, we squash people's curiosity and, even more sadly, crush our own into oblivion. What ever happened to our natural flexibility and ever-changing personalities and opinions? How did we become so stagnant?

If you find that your curiosity is gone or waning, don't fear. A life of really and truly expressing yourself—for who you are and what you feel in the moment—is always possible. Take a deep breath and try this exercise:

1. Close your eyes and decide to be genuinely curious about being curious.
2. Just like a child, let yourself connect with your wonderfully inquisitive mind.
3. Remember how it felt to ask questions with the inner spark of a fresh mind and a real yearning to discover new answers.
4. Remember being interested in the world around you and not being conditioned or restricted by an interpretation of how things *should* be.

Shake Free: Jumpstart Your Curiosity

You can jumpstart your rusty curiosity back into action in a very simple way: just stop, look, and listen. No matter how much knowledge you have stored in your brain, there are elements in life that are ever-changing and always fascinating. Feelings and personal opinions are never static. If we are willing to pay attention, we can easily feel ten different ways about a situation or a person, depending on how open we hold our heart to others and to ourself.

Stop. Look. Listen. When someone talks to you, make yourself stop and actually pay attention to what they are saying. As you look at them, realize that what they are saying is something they may have never thought, felt, or said before—it's a brand-new experience happening right now for them. Instead of interpreting what they say through your own points of view, ask clarifying questions—for example, "I am curious. What has you feel that way about that turn of events?"—and really listen to their responses. Give them your genuine attention, and they'll most likely give you new insight! People have very interesting things to say, if we are willing to listen to them instead of the busy chatter of our own mind.

You Can Do It: Reclaim Your Natural, Magical Skill

To be curious—to really listen—is a magical skill you can reclaim. When you are truly curious, there is no judgment toward yourself or others; there is space, empathy, joy, and compassion. By being curious, you can experience people through their actions as well as their hopes, aspirations, and dreams. Receiving others with curiosity teaches us how to accept ourself exactly the way we are in the moment.

When you are training yourself to "re-learn" how to pay attention to someone who is speaking to you, make eye contact, slow down, be present in your body, and use the words "I am curious" before you ask a question. I am invested in your being curious about *you*, so in one of today's exercises, you will interview yourself. You will ask yourself questions through which you will discover what is different *now*—now that you have let go of the paralyzing power of your stories, now that you are coming from a more authentic place of presence, and now that you are listening to the nuances of your feelings. There is nothing more rewarding than truly being curious about yourself and others. It opens up a new world of listening, where true vision and purpose come through bright and clear. It's as if you're talking to and listening to someone's essence or soul—the real person, rather than who you think they are.

We have ears and yet often don't listen. We have eyes and often see only what we want to see. Curiosity is about connecting with our body in a natural and profound way so that we can listen from our senses and not from our interpretations. Curiosity allows us to hear, see, experience people for who they are, not just who we think they are.

It's True: Life Is Invariably Messy

Very often, life seems to hit us with its messiness at the most inopportune moment.

As the famous saying goes, "Life is what happens when you're busy making other plans." We whine, "Everything would be just great if this didn't happen," and then collapse into self-pity because our perfect picture has disappeared and that challenges our comfort zone. We are in a complete mess, right? Wrong! It's actually easier than you may think to turn any situation around. When you connect with your curiosity, you are able to reassess everything with a new perspective and dance in the moment, without drama. With your original and wide-eyed curiosity, you can dig diligently through the messy details and find a creative solution to any situation or problem.

It may be hard to believe this from the comfort of your cocoon, yet it is true. In everything that happens to you, there is opportunity for growth—when you are authentically fascinated with life. Even in life's most surprising moments, if you are willing to stay open, you will see a treasure in everything.

Every interaction brings us an opportunity to let go of our smallness and stand in a place of spaciousness—where we can be Big. Fall in love with yourself through your curiosity about what motivates you and makes you click. Fall in love with yourself and the people in your life by listening to them with new ears and by looking out at life with new and curious eyes.

WORKBOOK: Day 6

DATE: D / M / Y

Reclaiming Your Curiosity

Recall a time in your life when you were truly curious. Connect with that moment and bring its vividness into the present. Describe it here.

Think about your Big Picture. What about it makes you most curious?

What do you think is the most valuable gift of curiosity? How do you feel when you are purely curious?

When you think about the goals that you have set to move toward your Big Picture, your heart's desire, what is it about those goals that makes you curious?

Re-Learning How to Listen

When you ask yourself the following questions, slow down, look yourself in the eye, and actually listen to the voice of your heart.

Who are you in this moment?

What makes you curious about yourself?

DAY 7

ACKNOWLEDGE YOUR PARACHUTE: YOUR LIFE STARTS NOW...JUMP!

A parachute is a metaphorical landing apparatus that protects us when we leap forward and jump fully into life. Our individual parachute is held together by all the work we've done in addressing the basic areas of our life: our education, our inner journey, our health, our finances, our professional experiences, our relationships with ourself and others, and our physical and emotional bodies.

Our parachute protects us from hurting ourself when we jump off cliffs, when we stretch our comfort zone by taking leaps forward, giant or tiny. Our parachute is our metaphorical lifesaving tool. A lot of us over-prepare for jumping into our life, to reduce risk; we never really leave our comfort zone, the parameters we have erected to guarantee our safety—and our stagnation. We never get to experience the strong, resilient parachute we have sewn for ourself, and admire the life we have created.

There is an epidemic going on in Western society. We are obsessed with living overly organized lives! We plan absolutely everything. We believe that failure is only negative and habitually over-prepare so we'll be equipped for every potential disaster. Emergency kits, back-up plans, exit strategies, safety nets—we are forgetting to actually live our life with a light heart and a trust in ourself. If you have those two attributes as a solid core, you will be able to handle any emergency that arises. You don't need to work so hard; life is easy. Have you ever entertained the idea that you've already sewn your parachute, the perfect one, to cushion any fall?

With your parachute on your back, you can confidently jump off most any cliff you choose. You are safe. Certainly, you can acquire more tools and resources as you age and grow, yet all there is to do to take the next step is to discern what knowledge you already have. Then, acknowledge your power and jump!

Guess What: The Future Is Now

One of my clients, Jill, has worked at her personal journey for many years and takes a bold, intense approach to her self-development. After a few months of my coaching, she told me she needed to make another "big leap" regarding her art career. As she defined her goals, I noticed she set them in the long-distant future. Jill wanted representation for her work in a nearby town and gave herself a year to acquire that. She wanted a website and gave herself six months to build one. With her goals in place, she told me she was preparing herself for a full, fantastic life six months down the road. Here was a bright, talented, healthy woman choosing to put her current fantastic life on hold...until her website was complete, until her deal came through, until everything felt "right." While waiting for that consummate life to be delivered, she was perfectly willing to hold her breath.

In fact, Jill did stop living! The preparations for living the ideal life consumed her. I asked her to consider, "What would it feel like to start living your life now?" Yes, set goals to manifest your Big Picture, and then keep moving forward. How about getting to the juice of living life to the fullest *now?* No countdown. No rehearsal. No more waiting.

When Does Your New Life Start? (Now, of course.)

I love when my clients ask me whether I think they are ready to move forward. I always respond, "What do *you* think?" As my perplexed client pondered the answer for herself, she visualized herself flying. She described the beautiful view she saw after taking off, the view from "up there," and how she was beginning to feel her own power. I reminded her that with all her years of intensive inner work, she had already sewn herself an enormous parachute. Finally owning that, she dove even deeper into her vision, saying, "I do have a parachute; I have been sewing one for so long!" She breathed a sigh of relief as she realized that she already had what she needed right there inside herself: the ability to fly high, boldly, and safely. If she was going to drop to the ground, she would be protected by her own, already consciously designed life.

Thrilled with this realization that she would land on her feet no matter what, Jill jumped into her present life and acknowledged the fact that not only had she sewn her own parachute, she had done a great job of it. This thought empowered her to feel confident in her ability to take care of herself. Jill took a deep breath and surrendered; she dropped the practice of over-preparing and skydived right into life.

A few hours after our session, a website designer had contacted her via e-mail to see if she was interested in launching her website. Life had taken on an air of synchronicity. Jill was delighted, feeling that her timing was perfect and her dance with life was happening…in the now.

Time-Out: Take an Inventory of Your Life and Assess Your Parachute

Does Jill's story sound familiar? Have you forgotten how hard you've worked to create your current life? Take an inventory of your life and assess your parachute. This is the place to be a discerning adult, because you will not be able to judge the appropriate height of your next jump if you do not accurately assess and test your parachute. Start by checking in with these questions:

- *How old am I?*

- *How are my finances?*

- *What is my relationship like with myself?*

- *How am I with other people?*

- *Is my education adequate to reach my goals?*

- *How is my physical health?*

- *How do I express my creativity?*

- *How ready am I to jump with my parachute?*

As you answer these questions, make sure you are your own barometer of success. Do not use some else's standards.

Lastly, ask yourself this: *What if the fear of falling is actually the excitement of flying?*

WORKBOOK: Day 7

DATE: D   /   M   /   Y

Assessing and Strengthening Your Parachute

What excuses do you make that prevent you from living your life to the fullest?

How is the state of your parachute with respect to your new goals and your Big Picture? Honestly assess where you stand in your present life and determine what updates need to be made in any of the following areas to obtain your goals:

- Education

- Finances

- Professional work

- Relationship with yourself

- Relationships with others

- Physical body

- Emotional body

- Spirituality

- Creativity

- Atmosphere you want to create right now

- Other areas of importance to you

Who would you be right now if you fully trusted your parachute?

DAY 8

DEFINE YOUR STEPS:
PUT YOURSELF IN CHARGE OF YOUR DESTINY

You are the creator of your own reality. You are the architect of your life. I'd be a millionaire if I had a dollar for every person who wants to win the lottery yet never buys a lottery ticket. Whether you buy a ticket or not is *your* choice. Putting yourself in charge of your own destiny—by clarifying your Big Picture, declaring your goals, and defining your steps toward those goals—is also your choice. Understand that life, *your* life, is a matter of cause and effect. If you seriously want something bad enough, you *can* make it happen. You have the power to win the lottery; start by buying the tickets!

Don't wait for your dream to happen to you. Make it happen by taking the necessary steps. Every day, we have the potential to win—because we get to choose who we want to be in our life. Isn't this freedom a better prize than winning a pile of cash? Okay, so you probably still want the cash; however, remember, you win the metaphorical lottery every day simply because you are alive. You get to choose who you want to be in your world, in your life, and to take the empowering actions that give your life meaning. You have the power to make your own life be the way you want it to be.

Congratulations for completing the first week of this manual. Congrats on your intention to design a conscious life for yourself. Now it's time to design the steps that you'll need to take to reach your goals. During this process, always keep your Big Picture, your goals, and your life purpose in mind while envisioning the unique atmosphere that will best support your forward movement.

Step Around It: Your Limited Thinking Is Your Biggest Obstacle

Defining the steps to achieve your goals is a very fun and fulfilling process, for which you really have to look at the aspects you so carefully addressed this past week. Go back and review your work of the last seven days—as many times as you want. You may have already inadvertently defined some of your steps in one of the earlier chapters, for example, while assessing your parachute or while creating the atmosphere that supports your goals.

Let go of any judgment that might arise, and remember, you can always redefine, rework, and deepen your earlier work. The point of today's exercise is to truly let go of your limiting thinking so that you can design your own best-case scenario. If you notice self-judgment as you review your answers from last week, ask yourself these four questions to stay on top of your thinking process:

- *Is this thought really true?*
- *How do I treat myself when I have this thought?*
- *Who would I be without this thought?*
- *Who would I be if the opposite was true?*

Your limited thinking is your biggest obstacle, so be aware of it every time you have a thought that brings you out of the perfect reality that is your life. As you'd practiced on Day 4, you can now consciously choose which thoughts best serve you. If one thought creates a wonderful frame of mind and the opposite thought fills you with self-doubt, the choice seems to be an easy one. There is no right or wrong, however; simply be aware of your conscious choices to hold on to thoughts or to let them go. You get to choose what you do with the thoughts that keep you from moving forward.

Create Steps: Relate Them to Your Big Picture and Goals

Work at defining your steps from a place of unlimited possibilities, where anything is possible. Simply notice if you can stay in that Big creative place and for how long. The following example is how one of my clients completed this chapter's exercise. Keep in mind that your Big Picture generates a feeling state that not only is important to you; it also defines your experience.

What is your Big Picture?

- *I have full trust in myself that I can be at the right place at the right time.*
- *I feel fully confident in my decision-making process.*
- *I wake up happy and excited to go to work.*

What are your goals related to your Big Picture? (Note: The goals below relate only to the third value above.)

- *To make more money*
- *To have a job in which I can experience confidence*
- *To be appreciated by a company that shares my values*

What steps do you need to take to reach your goals?

- *If I decide to look for a new job, I will need to:*
  - ✓ *update my resume.*
  - ✓ *solicit more references.*
  - ✓ *research companies that share my values.*
  - ✓ *send out 3 résumés a week.*
  - ✓ *have my interviewing outfit ready.*

- *If I decide to seek a new position where I currently work, I will need to:*
    - ✓ *define what sort of job with my current company could be my ideal job.*
    - ✓ *define what steps to take to qualify for that job.*

It's easy to think that in your professional life, for example, it's the job that is wrong. Perhaps it's the company, your boss, or the fact that your office is not big enough. From a place of curiosity, catch yourself making excuses and unconscious judgments. Now that you are clearer about yourself and committed to consciously taking charge of your life with your new and improved attitude, take a step back and ask yourself if the job you currently hold could be the ideal job. What needs to shift to make it the ideal job?

Honestly assess what is working and not working about where you currently are—coming from a place of observation, with no blame. If you find enough redeeming elements in your current situation, notice how you can make it work even better just by shifting your perception. From this vantage point of your new outlook on life, ask yourself what steps you need to take to get you where you want to be. Then take those steps and give your current situation a fair chance. If you find that your current situation does not fulfill you, then it's time to define the steps that will align your actions with what makes your heart sing.

No Excuses: Your New Life Is a Place of Clarity, Aligned with Your Big Picture

In the above example, it would be easy to blame the boss, job, or setting for creating a less-than-ideal situation—and to get others to agree with her. We love to find excuses and point fingers. We do the same in our relationships. We're so quick to label our friends, intimate partners, and relatives as being wrong. We think that moving on and leaving them behind is the best way to get to a new life— and then we find ourself in our "new" life experiencing the same situation over and over, with new partners, friends, and relatives.

Just in this first week, you have made tremendous shifts within yourself: you are clearer about your direction, your responsibilities, and your thought process. Coming from this new perception of yourself, assess your personal relationships. The only person you are in charge of is yourself, and the only person who can change is you. Instead of pointing fingers, decide what steps you can take to shift your thinking to self-accountability. If you are the maker of your own reality, then you are the maker of your own experience in your relationships. No one can hold you hostage unless you let him or her.

Our happiness is not contingent on what other people do or don't do. We are the maker of our own happiness, and we have the power to attract circumstances that forward our fulfillment. Don't give your power away by thinking that someone else can cause you misery or unhappiness; you do that to yourself. When you take charge of your life and accept that you are the conscious and powerful maker of your world and your circumstances, the universe opens up and responds to your intentionality with support. Out of the blue, people and other resources will show up to help you achieve your goals toward your Big Picture.

Before you move on to today's exercise, review my client's example and another common situation below:

Big Picture (Note: This is only one of the three values.):

- *I live a physically healthy life, not worrying about high cholesterol, and experience the confidence of taking good care of my body.*

Goals:

- *To lower bad cholesterol level*
- *To lower fat percentage*
- *To be more fit*

Steps:

- *Design a food plan that suits my diet concerns.*
- *Read more books about nutrition.*
- *Find a walking partner.*
- *Walk every day.*
- *Lift weights 3 times a week.*

WORKBOOK: DAY 8

DATE: D   /   M   /   Y

Creating Your Steps

What is your Big Picture? (Revisit Day 1 work pages.)

Write down the most urgent of your goals related to your Big Picture. (Revisit Day 2 work pages.)

What steps do you need to take to reach this goal? Be as specific and comprehensive as possible.

Record another one of your goals that you defined on Day 2.

What steps do you need to take to reach this goal?

Record another goal you defined on Day 2.

What steps do you need to take to reach this goal?

Prioritize your steps as short-term or long-term. First decide which goals you want to accomplish by the end of Day 30, and schedule their steps backward from Day 30. For each step, specify the date you would like to complete it by, write that date next to the step above, and then record the step on the first of the chapter-end work pages corresponding to its completion date.

If any of your goals exceed 30 days, record the post-30-day steps and their completion dates in the extra pages at the back of this book. You may also record other goals and their attendant steps there, too.

How do you want to feel in the process of actualizing your steps? For example, do you want to feel trusting? Happy? Fun? Serious? Grounded? Light-hearted? Concise? Clear? Confident? Optimistic?

You decide! Whatever feelings support the steps to achieve your goals are perfect for you. List them all; don't hold back.

Day 9

Become the Observer: Step Out of the Drama and Assess Without Judgment

Blaming outside circumstances, holding others responsible for our experience, and being ruled by old stories can generate a state in which we fall victim to the drama we have actually created. Drama is a diversion that keeps us busy and not moving forward. When drama is center stage, it absorbs all our attention such that we leave important life tasks incomplete, resulting in our failure to live our life to its fullest. Today, nine days into becoming the *new you*, you will learn how to recognize the drama in your life that holds you back. You will have the choice to just say no to drama!

Habitually, we create drama by fuelling gossip, dwelling in interminable thought loops, or continuing to participate in dead-end situations, whether a job or a relationship. We entangle our mind in a web of ultimately inconsequential details, clouding our long-range vision and sidetracking our self-direction. We idly concern ourself with others' behavior and circumstances so that we don't have to look at ourself, and we unnecessarily worry about people's reactions, thinking we can manage their perceptions of us.

We additionally feed our self-perpetuating drama by projecting ourself into a future of worst-case scenarios constructed from our assumptions. Being preoccupied by our drama makes it impossible to get centered, keep the focus on ourself, and live our life in the present moment.

Today, you will distinguish and learn to let go of the self-generated drama that takes you away from being powerful. Begin now by making a conscious choice to stop talking about other people and interpreting their actions and feelings. You do not know what they think or what motivates them. You are only in charge of yourself, and it is your task to wake up to what you think and what motivates *you*. Living in reaction to your assumptions, speculations, and perceptions about other people is a huge waste of time!

Be a Lighthouse: Stand Tall and Get Clear about Yourself

When we define our priorities, our values, and our heart's desire, and set our goals accordingly, we create a life of integrity, and everything else falls into place like magic. We dilute our power of intention when we constantly focus on others, whether in judgment or in fear of their reaction. Leave other people's business to them, and your life will flourish and bloom. Take care of your own business, and grant others your trust that they know what is best for their lives, whether you agree with their choices or not. You will be surprised by how much energy you will preserve for yourself if you are not minding other people's business.

You are not here to judge or criticize; you are here to observe. Today, consciously become the Observer of your own world. You will find yourself in a majestic position: from this place of gentle clarity and command, you can stay grounded as you assess your past, your future, and especially the present moment. This way of perceiving—being the Observer—enables you to make empowering choices with integrity, that is, aligned with who you are, your goals, and your Big Picture.

When learning to observe, consider the metaphor of the lighthouse. The lighthouse represents security in its permanence and immobility. Its job is to stand tall and visible, allowing onlookers to decide which direction to take. Likewise, the job of your Observer is to be an objective, ever-present source of knowledge illuminating your options for action. You stand tall in your intention to take care of your business and yourself, no matter the actions or reactions of anyone else.

When we come from integrity and conscious choice, we naturally transcend worrying about others. We move into a place of surrender and allow them their own opinions. Too much time and energy is wasted in this world making decisions either to please others or to preclude their potential reactions. When we stand tall and firmly planted in our own integrity, we increase the likelihood that people will receive us with open arms.

Find the metaphor that inspires you to detox from misplaced worry and other unnecessary drama. If the lighthouse metaphor doesn't work for you, you might imagine yourself on top of a mountain, a skyscraper, or any place from which you can objectively survey your entire life or specific circumstances. Evaluate yourself and your goals truthfully, and use that calm, clear, and composed appraisal to revise your current plan wherever a modification will better serve your heart's desire.

Let Go: Walk a Clear Path to Where You Want to Go

I know what you are capable of. Do you? Chances are, I see you as more resourceful than you see yourself. I trust that you are able to let go of anything that stands in the way of where you want to go and who you want to be. Do you have this kind of confidence in yourself? I have worked with enough people to know that, as human beings, we are naturally creative, resourceful, and whole. We each have an innate capacity to open our ears and listen to our inner voice—the voice that tells us what is good for us and how to get there.

As human beings, we each also have an inherent vision that suddenly opens our eyes to the path we must take to fully and authentically express ourself. We know who we were born to be. We are complete human beings, with all our great qualities and great imperfections, holding the knowledge of where we stand at all times and which choices we want to make.

From this place of deep awareness, there is never a right or wrong choice. There is only what you know will make you happy in the present moment. By consciously attending to yourself, to *your* happiness rather than that of others, you will make the world a happier place. You don't serve anyone—yourself, your relationships, the world—by hiding or denying who you are.

Witnessing your whole life through the Observer's lens is one of the most radical changes you can make for yourself. You can observe how drama feeds itself through overreaction—overthinking, overtalking, overanalyzing, overgossiping— and how it slows you down or stops you. You can then recognize your power in choosing to disrupt that pattern and take a different action, one that supports you regardless of other people's opinions and reactions. You can view your goals with detached objectivity and design your steps from that clarity. When you intentionally observe yourself and others from a higher perspective—and consciously choose to take ownership of your well-being and the fulfillment of your heart's desire—you let go of victimization and judgment. You view the world through benevolent eyes and see the gifts in every person and in every experience. When you do this, the rest of the world sees and embraces you with the same warm and benevolent eyes.

WORKBOOK: Day 9

DATE: D / M / Y

Observing Your Drama

What drama stands in the way of your achieving your goals?

What do you get from being hooked into this drama?

Are you willing to let go of this drama? Who would you be without this drama?

What do you need to do to be free to focus on your goals instead of this drama? The Observer always stands in clarity. What is standing in the way of your clarity?

How do you feel when you identify yourself as the Observer?

What's your next step? Discard other people's notions of what you should be and do, and regroup within yourself. Who are YOU and what do YOU want?

DAY 10

REWORK YOUR RECIPE:
KEEP WHAT WORKS AND CHANGE WHAT DOESN'T

Life is about regularly assessing what works and what doesn't, and updating our system. It's about determining the beliefs we want to hold on to, and distinguishing what has worked in the past to get us what we want. From that place of discernment, we can keep revising our life formula, our recipe for success.

Instead of judging your past mistakes and accomplishments, look back on your life objectively: you will attain a more accurate assessment of what worked and what didn't work for you. When you've set goals in the past, or declared big aspirations, or launched sizeable projects, what were the defining elements that successfully moved you toward the actualization of your objectives? What was your approach? Does it work for you to make lists? To hire someone who holds you accountable? To have a well-defined plan? To dance in the moment? How do you maintain your optimism and flexibility when you encounter adversity? How do you continue to have fun and enjoy the ride, in spite of the bumps?

Many of us think we have to "know it all" and "do it all" in life. Is this 100% true? What is true is that when we believe this thought, we often don't allow ourself to reach out for help. There are a wide variety of professionals who can support us in achieving our goals with ease. For example, when a client who wanted to be fit planned her ideal fitness regime, she didn't consult or hire a personal trainer. Instead, she held firmly to her unquestioned notion that she *should* know how to be fit, and consequently, she never reached her goal.

Ask Yourself:
Who Is Holding Me Accountable?

My clients tell me that my holding them accountable to their agenda is worth the money they pay me to be their coach. They reach their goals on time, often earlier, and when they don't meet their target, they learn tremendously from the process and apply that experience to their ensuing efforts. While I would love to work with you, the reader, as your coach, ultimately what I am saying is that hiring a professional may be helpful for you.

Is holding on to the conviction that you have to "know it all" and "do it all" working for you? Set aside any money concerns and ask yourself, *Who would I be if I admitted that I need help? What would I gain if I hired the right professional to support me in reaching my goals?* Do you need an accountant, an investor, a matchmaker, a lawyer? If your current resources are not supporting you, ask yourself if it is time to get outside help.

In addition to professional allies, who in your personal sphere can hold you accountable to your vision? Who in the past has supported you in word and deed, and who has sabotaged your efforts? Remember to assess with the Observer's eye, without judgment, so that you can write your own recipe for success that serves who you want to be and where you want to go, regardless of others' viewpoints.

Before Evaluating the Past, Remember Your Alliance with Yourself

On Day 4, you discerned the ways you do, and could, treat yourself when things do and do not go according to plan. This process of assessing what has and hasn't worked in the past is an opportunity not to berate yourself but to help define the atmosphere that is most conducive to the realization of your goals.

Reassess what you may have deemed a failure in the past as a lesson in understanding what doesn't work for you. Allow some flexibility in evaluating, as every situation is different. Trust that all experiences are designed to serve your Biggest self, and this simple shift in your perception will enable you to extract the invaluable education that learning by contrast provides.

Reworking your recipe for success is a time to marvel at your innate capacity to push your comfort zone, to adapt and be flexible, and to find energy in every challenge and circumstance of your exciting life.

WORKBOOK: DAY 10

DATE: D / M / Y

Observing Your Drama

What has worked in the past to support you in reaching your goals?

What, if anything, had you judged as a failure? Review each situation without judgment and discover its lesson. Can you reach your goals by yourself? Honestly assess whether you could use professional support. If so, define the areas in which you could use assistance.

Coming from possibility rather than resignation and excuses, what do you need to put in place so that you can receive assistance? Consider whether you would have to rearrange your schedule, or, in order to afford professional guidance, save or borrow money or prioritize your spending.

What kind of personal support system do you need to put in place? Identify the key people in your life with whom you can share your vision and, specifically, how they can help you reach your goals. If you are trying to lose weight, for example, you might ask those in your household to not buy junk food.

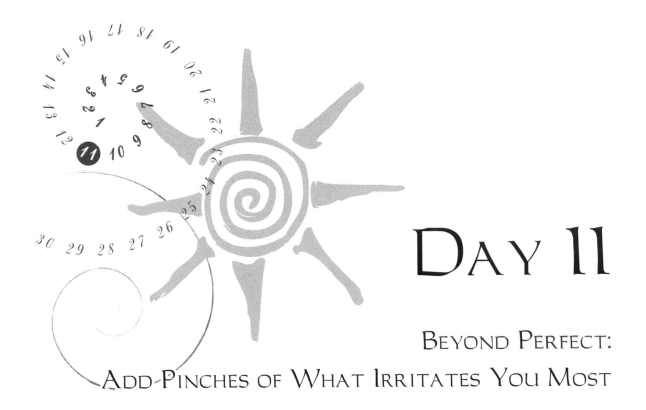

DAY 11

BEYOND PERFECT:
ADD PINCHES OF WHAT IRRITATES YOU MOST

We live in a world that has conditioned us to think that in order to be loved and appreciated, we can only show or admit our good qualities. To be fully accepted, then, we learn to hide attributes judged as "bad." This habitual strategizing exhausts us and entraps us in a collective agreement of social propriety and conformity, devaluing the very authenticity that deepens genuine love and appreciation. Today, let's move "beyond perfect" and on to what's really real.

 Does perfection mean that we can't have any "bad" qualities, that we always have to be in a good mood or behave positively? We are already perfect in who we are—wonderful beings with multifaceted personalities. We each are a multitude of attributes composing our unique individuality. We need to discard the "or"—in right or wrong, light or dark, them or us—and see what shifts in the world when we replace "or" with "and."

Good and bad. Right and wrong. Up and down. Sad and happy. We are different in our traits, essences, and feelings; each one of us is a delightful combination of qualities held together by "and." We are perfect in our imperfections—so imagine this: we don't need to change; we already have all we need. Accept all that you are without judgment. Accept and integrate all your characteristics and qualities, even the ones you have judged, ignored, disconnected from, or pretended you don't have.

Embrace your "shadow side": your composite of socially undesirable attributes, such as arrogant, bossy, self-centered, stubborn, jealous, and greedy. These qualities have a lot to teach you. When you acknowledge that you do, indeed, have a shadow side and that its qualities also are part of your emotional DNA, you can surrender to your humanness and realize that these qualities help to make you *you*. Without them, you would be incomplete, a monotoned Stepford wife. Denying these qualities, you would be unfulfilled, as they are essential elements of your makeup, of your authentic self. Your shadow-side qualities and your sunny-side-up qualities all work to support you in constructive ways.

Live Your Life Uniquely Imperfect

Each one of us is perfectly unique in our imperfections; our flaws define us as the distinct person we individually are. Living life "beyond perfect" is a stance, another radical act you can commit, starting today, on your journey to the *new you*. It's about honoring who you really are, instead of pretending or striving to be who you think you should be or wish you could be. Any presentation to the world other than who you really are is inauthentic and depletes your energy.

Living life beyond perfect is about abandoning your projection of perfection as a prescribed formula and embracing your multicolored individuality, the dark and the light. Yes, you can be arrogant and compassionate at the same time, when you allow all that you are. And when you accept and integrate your dark and light qualities, you can powerfully move toward who you want to be: the fulfilled you of your Big Picture. Give yourself and others the opportunity to enjoy your magnificent, glorious, courageous, and sometimes moody, irreverent, silly self in all your authentic essence!

When we focus strictly on the positive, on perfection, or on a utopian existence, we express only half of our being. When we don't sink into the cavernous depths of our rich, multilayered personality, we can't experience our full aliveness. In today's exercise, you will assess some of the attributes considered negative, by most people, in order to discover their positive essences and determine how "pinches" of shadow attributes can be used to your advantage to achieve your goals.

Mirror, Mirror: Take a Long, Kind Look

This is the time to be totally honest, to first indulge your judgment and then stretch and look again from a place of observing rather than judging. Boldly enter the areas you find difficult to look at. This is where you will find the greatest rewards for yourself.

Fully embraced, every quality has an essence that can support us. The qualities we need to most embrace in ourself are the ones we dislike in other people. Ah, the miraculous work of the mirror! Today's exercise will help you detect those qualities that trigger you and thereby run your life from an unconscious place. Remember, there is treasure in everything, and accepting that you are beyond perfect is one of the most courageous and self-loving moves you can make—which, in turn, makes you more accepting of others' imperfections.

By owning your unique complexity, you hold yourself Big and accountable for fully claiming your life. For each one of us, the journey of self-discovery and acceptance has a unique timetable and a unique set of obstacles and signposts, yet we share an innate ability to rise until we're standing on our own two feet and to walk that journey until we're dancing. When we make choices with the undistorted vision of our true, "beyond perfect" self, we can be sure that we are creating an authentic life, aligned with our values, our goals, our heart's desire.

WORKBOOK: Day 11

Date: D / M / Y

Assessing Your Attributes

There are three distinct steps to finding the treasure in an attribute:

1. Write down the attribute that irritates or triggers you.

2. Record the negative connotations of this attribute. (This is your opportunity to really indulge your annoyance and be judgmental).

3. Become the Observer, your unbiased and curious self, and reinterpret the attribute from this perspective, looking to uncover its positive essences.

In the following pages, I model the process for several attributes, using examples from my clients, so that you can successfully engage in your own process.

Attribute: arrogant

Negative Connotations	Positive Essences
Arrogant people: • Are full of themselves • Talk about themselves too much • Make themselves bigger than they are • Always think they are right • Don't care about others' opinions	*Arrogant people:* • Are self-confident • Don't gossip about others • Are bold individuals • Have no self-doubt • Focus on themselves

Now define your own negative connotations and positive essences for the attribute of arrogant.

Your Negative Connotations	Your Positive Essences

How can a pinch of the positive essence of **arrogance** *get you to your goals faster?*

Where can you be more bold, self-confident, internally focused, and certain in your life?

Attribute: selfish

Negative Connotations	Positive Essences
Selfish people: • Only consider themselves • Do not reciprocate equally • Are demanding • Don't worry about others • Don't consider others	*Selfish people:* • Are self-sufficient • Don't sacrifice themselves • Know what they want • Have more freedom • Are accountable for themselves

Your Negative Connotations	Your Positive Essences

*How can you use a pinch of the positive essence of **selfishness** to reach your goals?*

Where in your life can you be more free, self-sufficient, clear about what you want, and accountable for yourself?

Attribute: bossy

Negative Connotations	Positive Essences
Bossy people: • Only consider themselves • Do not reciprocate equally • Are demanding • Don't worry about others • Don't consider others	*Bossy people:* • Are self-sufficient • Don't sacrifice themselves • Know what they want • Have more freedom • Are accountable for themselves

Your Negative Connotations	Your Positive Essences

*How can a conscious pinch of the positive essence of **bossiness** help you move forward?*

Where can you be more committed, resourceful, decisive, and trusting in your own decision-making process regardless of any opposition?

Attribute: boastful

Negative Connotations	Positive Essences

Boastful people:
• Are full of themselves
• Are arrogant
 	
• Are self-centered
 	
• Toot their own horn
	• *Boastful people:*
	  • Trust their own capabilities
	  • Believe they can do anything
	  • Assume that everyone can take care of themselves
	  • Advocate for themselves

Your Negative Connotations	Your Positive Essences

If you let go of judging this attribute, you'll see that the positive essence of boastfulness can help a person really sell him/herself. When you genuinely think the world of yourself, it's easy to sing your praises from a place of fulfillment.

How can a conscious pinch of the positive essence of **boastfulness** *help you realize your Big Picture?*

How would it feel to sing your own praises with authentic trust in your capabilities, promoting yourself and holding a positive regard about who you are and your accomplishments?

Now pick some attributes that really irritate or trigger you and, following the process, record your negative connotations and positive essences for each one. Then assess how a pinch of that attribute can support you in reaching your goals faster.

Remember, you can come back to this process whenever you are irritated in your life and transform the irritation into a treasure. Here are the three steps again:

1. Write down the attribute that irritates or triggers you.

2. Record the negative connotations of this attribute. (This is your opportunity to really indulge your annoyance and be judgmental.)

3. Become the Observer, your unbiased and curious self, and reinterpret the attribute from this perspective, looking to uncover its positive essences.

Attribute:

Your Negative Connotations	Your Positive Essences

How, and in which areas of your life, can a pinch of the positive essence of this attribute support you?

Attribute:

Your Negative Connotations	Your Positive Essences

How, and in which areas of your life, can a pinch of the positive essence of this attribute support you?

Attribute:

Your Negative Connotations	Your Positive Essences

How, and in which areas of your life, can a pinch of the positive essence of this attribute support you?

Attribute:

Your Negative Connotations	Your Positive Essences

How, and in which areas of your life, can a pinch of the positive essence of this attribute support you?

Attribute:

Your Negative Connotations	Your Positive Essences

How, and in which areas of your life, can a pinch of the positive essence of this attribute support you?

Attribute:

Your Negative Connotations	Your Positive Essences

How, and in which areas of your life, can a pinch of the positive essence of this attribute support you?

Day 12

Strong + Weak = You: Learn to Work Together

Today, we'll explore how both our strong and weak points can work for us. From the curious place of the Observer, we'll extend Day 11's notion that a conscious pinch of all attributes makes us well-rounded and definitely more interesting! Basically, you'll be working to integrate your weaknesses with, and see them as valuable as, your strengths. Today, be bold. Commit to love the so-called bad with the good, the so-called weak with the strong: the whole, complex, delicious you.

Today, make a conscious choice to throw away all limiting conceptions, personal and societal, that dictate what is strong and what is weak, what is good and what is bad. Let go of judgment and duality for one day and just see what happens: no good or bad, no right or wrong, no positive or negative. Instead, today you will look at each of your attributes and ask yourself, *How does this serve me, and how can it serve me better?* This assessment will require you to be in the present moment, simply noticing, neutral to any opinions and prejudices you may have.

Start Strong: What Do You Do Well?

In today's exercise, you will explore all the things you know you are good at, with respect to the steps you've committed to take to achieve the goals that compose your Big Picture. Are you good at making lists or following directions? Are you naturally good with people? Are you an independent innovator or a trusty team player? Is communication one of your innate skills? Is your preferred medium writing or speaking?

Then you will assess what you perceive to be the weak points of your personality, with respect to your steps and goals. Notice your self-judgments and gently let them go. You can make this fun, you know—people like being around people who can laugh at themselves!

So, are you a procrastinator? What is the positive essence of that? You know there has to be one! How can it serve you to use a conscious pinch of this positive essence of procrastination: the commitment to live life on your own schedule? Another positive essence of procrastinators is that they make their present moment's desire more important than anything else.

Do you jump to conclusions too quickly? What is the positive essence of that? For today's exercise, remember to take your time as you explore this question from a place of neutrality. Might the positive essence of jumping to conclusions be a developed sense of intuition? How can it serve you to use a conscious pinch of intuition as you create your life? It will help to imagine consciously using each positive essence of the attributes you judge as your weaknesses to see how it serves you.

Own It: Your Strengths—and Weaknesses, Too!

Become the conscious owner of all your qualities—strong and weak—by simply embracing your totality, your wholeness. When people tell you that you are "too much" of something, it's likely that they are uncomfortable with the magnitude of that attribute. Remember, you are a mirror for them, as they are for you. If you consciously or unconsciously agree with another's judgment, it's usually because you yourself judge that attribute as bad. Once you clean up your beliefs around your attributes, others' reactions to you will not affect you. And the funny thing about the mirror is that once you stop judging yourself, others will stop, too!

Take a Deep Breath: Assess Yourself with Confidence

Knowledge of your weak points is invaluable information to have: you can utilize their positive essences to maximize your strengths as you work to realize your heart's desire. When you see yourself for your totality, you can objectively examine the disempowering aspects of your weaknesses to determine what to do about them. You may decide to read self-improvement literature addressing those areas or hire others to help you with certain tasks. Knowing and accepting your weaknesses actually empowers you, because your capacity to choose emerges when your self-judgment and resistance are no longer there.

Have fun discovering yourself with curious and compassionate eyes, as you welcome the magnificence of your wholeness!

WORKBOOK: Day 12

DATE: D / M / Y

Assessing Your Strengths and Weaknesses

List all the things you are good at. Keep your Big Picture, your goals, and your steps in mind.

List your weak points and then reinterpret them to find their positive essences.

Weak Points: Positive Essences:

How can these positive essences serve you in achieving your goals?

Now review your weaknesses with the Observer's eye focused on how they might hinder the steps you've mapped out to accomplish your goals. Make a specific plan for resolving these issues.

Day 13

Watch Your Language!
Empower Your Actions by What You Say

Limiting beliefs drive the excuses we use to not take the actions that would move us forward in our life. Often these thoughts are so unconsciously embedded in our psyche, in our being, that they affect our life with insidious consistency. As you shift into a *new you*, the easiest and most effective way to identify your hidden limiting beliefs is to pay attention to your language, because your speaking reflects your thinking.

Listen Up: What Holds You Back?

Starting today, watch your language. Or rather, listen closely to what you say. Every time you hear a "but" or an "I should" or an "I need to," you'll find a conditioned thought lurking behind your excuse or self-guilt trip. What does this type of language mean and how does it hold you back?

- BUT: "I wanted to run the marathon, *but* it was raining." You use this word when you want to blame something or someone else for your choice. It's a word that actually contradicts what you profess to want by symbolically negating every word that precedes it.

- SHOULD: "I *should* go visit my mother." When you hear yourself using this word, beware of becoming a victim. It's a word that conveys a sense of obligation rather than the willingness to act in accordance with your convictions and your authentic values and commitments. When you use "should," your body might show up for whatever you feel obligated to do, yet your authentic self will not be present.

- NEED TO: "I *need* to make more money." "I *need* to get married." Hear yourself using this phrase and you can be sure that you are lacking trust in your own resourcefulness and wholeness. "Need to" has more of a sense of desperation rather than of excitement. When you want to do something, that desire generates enthusiasm and motivates you to step into action. Accomplishing a "want" is more personally satisfying than completing something you "needed to" do.

Make a Shift: Change Your Speech Patterns

All my clients agree. One of the shifts that has most effectively helped them achieve fulfillment and greater consciousness is their stopping the use of these limiting words and replacing them with more empowering ones. For example, when we consciously replace "but" with "and," we realize instantly how multifaceted and complex we are, and we open to our unlimited potential. "I am very motivated, *but* sometimes I am lazy" becomes "I am very motivated, *and* sometimes I am lazy." "And" enables you to enjoy being a fabulous combination of things!

What would your experience be if you rephrased your "I should" and "I need to" sentences with "I want to" and a huge exclamation mark? How would it sound? When we enthusiastically shout out "Yes!" we know we're standing in our authentic self—the self most empowered to move us forward. Give it a try: "I should go to the gym" becomes "I want to go to the gym!" Suddenly you feel empowered, not guilty. The negated version also works: "I don't want to go to the gym!" You make it very clear what you do not want, and you consciously grant yourself permission to not go.

When you do things out of a "need" or a sense of "should," you will resent it. While your intention may be to please people, they will, in fact, perceive your resentment and know you are acting out of obligation rather than conscious choice. Obligation feels like pressure. Forcing yourself to do things is a surefire way to *not* get the results you want.

Listen Again: What Delays Your Present?

People genuinely enjoy us when we are motivated by passion and come from an authentic place of being. Language that disowns our personal accountability and power to choose leaves us unmotivated, not present, and joyless. The weather, age, money, resistant or uncooperative loved ones—these are the excuses my clients use over and over to keep themselves from living authentically. Notice if and when you use them.

- Weather: The weather is always at one extreme or another. "It's too sunny, too rainy, too hot, too cold..."
- Age: The current age is always the wrong age to move forward. "I'm too young to be a CEO." "I'm too old to go back to school."
- Money: "I don't have enough money." Many of us use this one!
- Loved ones: A loved one is always in the way. "I really want to..., but my wife/husband..."

During this pivotal stage of watching your language, don't judge; just be the curious Observer. Acknowledge your willingness to do this meticulous work of investigating the tool you probably use most frequently and naturally—your speaking. You are learning from the best teacher anyone could have: *you.*

Head Games: How Old Is Your Heart?

I have noticed that age often plays a prominent role in the non-pursuit of goals, dreams, and big projects. How many times have you heard or said something to this effect: "I'm too old to start learning piano now." "I'm not old enough to get that promotion." "People my age just don't do that." "Sail around the world at my age?"

Whether it's "too old" or "too young," many of us regard our age as a liability—instead of as an asset—in the pursuit of our bigger and better goals. In most situations, it is attitude, not age, that determines our success in following our heart's desire. We can use anything to support ourself or to hold ourself back. It's just a matter of perspective.

As we near the completion of Week 2, realize that you've already done a lot of work to shift into a different perception of yourself. You've looked at the stories that run your life; you've practiced being the Observer; you've learned how to assess your thoughts and choose which ones to hold on to and which to let go. Now, with curiosity and fun, address those excuses you persistently use to not take action. Become aware of your language, and try to catch every "but," "should," and "need to" that exits your mouth. Each time you misspeak, rephrase your language so that you can experience the difference it makes and ingrain the new language into the *new you*.

WORKBOOK: DAY 13

DATE: D / M / Y

Examining Your Language

Revisit your goals and the steps you need to take to realize your heart's desire. What excuses do you use to not take action?

What are the biggest "should's" and "should not's" that have ruled you and your life?

(Examples: "I should know what's good for me." "Good girls shouldn't have this much fun." "I should be making more money than my wife." "Men shouldn't show their feelings.")

When you designed your goals on Day 2 and your steps on Day 8, did you do so from need or want? Go back and fully reassess your goals using your wants as the motivator. Record any revised goals and steps below, and prioritize and schedule them as you did on Day 8.

What would it be like to fully surrender to what you want?

DAY 14

YOUR ORIGINAL SPARK: THE FLAME THAT KEEPS YOU GOING

Your Original Spark is your core essence. If you peeled away all the layers—your roles, your image, your personas, your personality, all the things you think you are, all your identifying markers—you would be left in your core state. That core state is different for different people; it is a feeling state that defines the essence of you. For some of us, it is freedom: there is nothing we would rather feel than free. For others of us, it is passion or wholeness or peace. Life makes no sense unless we are experiencing that essence inside ourself.

Our life is wonderful when we are connected with our Original Spark. You know you have lost contact with your Spark when you ask, *Is this all there is to life?* You may find yourself deflated and mopey, thinking you've been ripped off. It is when we are caught up in the "doing" of our life, instead of living it with full awareness, that we find ourself out of touch with our essence, our Original Spark. We may have been out of touch with it for so long that we don't even remember we have it, let alone how it feels. Your Original Spark is what ignites your wants. It's what will electrify every moment of every day of your life if you're plugged into it.

Imagine what it would feel like to jump out of bed singing just because you can't wait to begin your day. If you are not awakening with the juice of being alive coursing through your veins, you may have lost your Original Spark—that particular essence you are here on earth to express. Don't worry; it's not lost forever, just misplaced or momentarily forgotten. Today, you will learn how to reconnect with your core state.

Tap Into It: Fire Up the Power of Your Spark

Often we are so caught up in our day-to-day duties that we forget what our motivations are. We go to work, unmindful of our Original Spark that made us want to go into a particular line of business in the first place. Your Original Spark is the "why" behind your wants. For example, say you started your own business so that you could, in addition to generating an income, do whatever you want to do whenever you want to do it. Your answer to the question "Why?"—*Why is this important to me? What feeling state does it provide me?*—would take you to your core essence, your Spark: freedom. If your dream has always been to make the world a better place, your answer to the question "Why?"—*Why is this important to me? What do I feel deep inside when I am making the world a better place?*—might be compassion.

Your Original Spark is yours; it dictates your reasons for being who you are and wanting what you want. In turn, you want what you want because you know it will connect you with your essence! Your Original Spark is truly sacred, which is why the experiences that connect you with it are sacred to you. It's too easy to get out of synch with that sacred energy, to get caught up in the nitty-gritty of the business of life and forget your Big Picture. Overcome any self-judgment and return to the simplicity, the sanctuary, of your core essence—and reconnect with the authentic you, the you who you were before you imposed all the limitations on yourself. You will never be profoundly happy until you do.

What Gets in the Way of Connecting with Your Spark?

Every time you have a limiting thought about yourself, you stomp out the flame of your Original Spark. One of the ways you do this is to punish yourself for not obtaining your desired results. Whether or not you achieve your goals doesn't define you; your Spark does. Failing at something doesn't make you a failure. You are infused with a particular essence, and that essence fuels your ambitions; the farther outside your comfort zone you play, the more likely you will fail. Failing points to your courage to play Big! It's an opportunity to learn, and you can use the new information and insights to confirm or clarify what you want and the steps to get it. A life played well and fully experienced guarantees occasional failing. When you recognize that you are not your failures, you can pick yourself up with pride and celebrate your essential self.

Make a List: What Do You Want?

Now take a moment to relax and inhale a deep full breath, filling your body with the atmosphere of your Original Spark. Envision your life in synch with that fire. How would it affect you? How would it affect the people around you? When you are happy and dancing, the entire world dances with you.

Today, you will make a list of all the benefits you and those around you will experience as a result of your living your life, both personal and professional, connected with your Original Spark. This list will be the firewood for your Original Spark. Be proud of this list; be specific and bold about the benefits you want yourself and others to experience. Then keep this list where you can easily find it, so that whenever you're discouraged, feeling lost, or at a crossroads, you can review your list. You'll find that your spirits will lift just by reading it.

Infuse Your Goals with Your Original Spark: Who Do You Become?

Who are you when you are connected with your Spark? Who are you when you are living your life with full intention and your inner fire is fueled by your essence? Who are you when your dream isn't a dream anymore; it's your reality? Today, you will revisit the goals you set on Day 2 and infuse them with your Original Spark so that you are powerfully and authentically working toward the realization of your Big Picture.

Now that we're at the halfway mark, something I said on Day 1 bears repeating: *30 Days to a New You* is not for the faint of heart. This work is for those who want to live an extraordinary life that leaves their unique mark on others and the world. This work is for those who can acknowledge their fear and move ahead anyway, who can rejoice in their mistakes, and who can honor their essence. When you are connected to your Original Spark, nothing weighs you down; nothing dilutes your power. Fan the flame that ignites you and watch your life light up!

WORKBOOK: DAY 14

DATE: D / M / Y

Defining Your Original Spark

Record what you want in each of these categories:

Personal Life   Professional Life

For each want, ask yourself, How is this important to me? What is its value to me?
What feeling state would this provide me if I had it?

Want: Importance/Value: Feeling State:

Your answers to the previous questions will reveal your core essence, your Spark. Don't be afraid to declare it below:

_____ *is my Original Spark.*

I am here on earth to express _____

Review the goals you defined on Day 2 and consciously infuse them with your Original Spark. Take your time. Envision yourself fully alive in your life, achieving your goals one after another.

List all the advantages, benefits, and rewards—both tangible and intangible—that you and the people around you will receive when you are living your life ignited by your Original Spark.

Day 15

Your Secret:
What You Most Defend From Others

We all have some secret we invest energy in to keep it hidden from others. We're convinced that revealing it will cause people to judge us as harshly as we judge ourself, perhaps to the point of abandoning us. We fear that our secret might nullify all our good qualities and actions. At the very least, our secret is something we're not proud of.

Regardless of its intensity, it takes a tremendous amount of energy to harbor a secret, the impact of which we're hardly aware. Our buried, long-held secrets hold hostage our authentic flow. They keep us very busy making sure—consciously or unconsciously—that no one ever discovers our secret and what it means about us.

What we resist persists! What we cannot accept about ourself will rule our life until we fully embrace both our shadow self and our light self. As long as we disown or conceal aspects of ourself, we remain in a "wounded child" state. Conversely, revealing our secrets and thus releasing their energy propels us into the adult state of accountability.

Even if we make millions of dollars every year, maintain productive relationships, and succeed in other aspects of the material world, we remain a poor fabrication of oursef if our energy is bound up in hiding our secrets because we believe they mean something terrible about us. When we make ourself transparent, we are free to be our rich, authentic self, proud to be in our own company. Suppressing our secret-bound aspects, while almost instinctual, costs us the fulfilled life of our Big Picture: that is, we pay for our secrets by living an unfulfilled, small or diminished life.

So why do we spend so much energy blocking our secrets from other people, and sometimes from our own consciousness? Is it the secret's content that we are driven to keep hidden, or the conclusion we have drawn about ourself as a participant in the event? In our mind, the two get collapsed. Concealing the secret means concealing the attendant conclusion about ourself. For example, if you lied to someone as a child, you may think you want to hide the fact that you lied, yet what carries the shame is actually what you've decided lying means about you: *If I lied, then who am I? Selfish? Immoral? Untrustworthy? A fraud?* Your interpretation depends on your specific unhealed self-belief. And if you allow yourself to feel the shame—the denial of which keeps that belief in place—you might discover that your crime doesn't equal the life sentence you have given yourself.

One of my clients, a successful therapist who deeply values honesty, revealed, during an emotional session, a secret she had never told anyone. Convinced that she had committed a horrific crime, she confessed to lying to her boyfriend when she was sixteen about being pregnant in order to get him back. Although she had succeeded, she condemned herself as a selfish liar, guilty for life. This belief was buried so completely that she couldn't even connect its significance with her current concern: she had hired me because she believed she couldn't be trusted in an intimate relationship. Likewise, what we believe about ourself, even if buried deep within, plays out in our present and will continue to impact us until we update that belief.

One of the most effective ways to correct a mistaken self-belief is to tell a safe person your secret and what you believe it means about you. For my client, this was very difficult to do because, as an adult, she would never consciously lie, and she was convinced that my respect for her would plummet. Still, she took the risk to tell me her secret; and I received her, reporting my feelings when she was done. I felt warmer toward her than before she had shared, and she was shocked! How could something she deemed so immoral and despicable actually engender connection and closeness?

It's simple, really. When you are invested in guarding a secret, it is difficult for others to fully experience you. When you drop your guard and share vulnerably what you suspect to be true about you, you are being authentic. Authentic vulnerability, both light and dark, always invites connection.

After that particular session, my client reported an increased level of energy and aliveness in all areas of her life, especially in her relationships. Her self-trust grew, and because it was now stripped of an outdated overlay of judgment, she could validate her trustworthiness in a healthy intimate relationship. She made peace with the fact that, at sixteen, she had done the best she could, considering her age and her resources. She even resolved that, without that past event, her value of honesty might not have crystallized into such a driving force in her life.

When you are willing to expose your secrets and the attendant self-beliefs, you will discover that judging, protecting, and hiding them is simply a waste of energy. In fact, the energy that you free up when you release your secrets will be essential in fueling your movement toward your goals.

WORKBOOK: Day 15

Date: D / M / Y

Investigating Your Secret and Your Resultant Self-Belief

What is the secret you least want to reveal to the world? Write it out in all its details.

(If you think that you are an open book with nothing to hide, that you don't have a secret belief about yourself, you may still be looking at yourself through the eyes of your guard. It's okay to lower your defenses and know that you will be safe in the pages of your own book.)

What does it mean about you that you were a participant in this event? What are you making that event mean about you? What is your self-judgment?

What practical reasons could explain your behavioral choice back then?

What do you need to do to be accountable for your actions in this event?

What current core values does this past event violate?

Seeing yourself clearly and compassionately through your adult eyes, opened further by this exploration, what is really true about you?

What is different about you now, standing in this truth?

How will you use your reclaimed energy to move you toward your goals?

DAY 16

SHARE YOUR SECRET: INVITE THE SUN TO SHINE

Discovering and coming to terms with a dark secret may be experienced by some of us as a moment of extreme liberation: we literally feel released. The more energy we have spent defending our secret, the bigger our emancipation. We may feel as though a tremendous weight has fallen off our shoulders, and we are relieved. Others of us might experience very different reactions. We may need more time to come to terms with it and, and even though we have no intention of sharing it yet, our confronting it has opened more space in our life. Because we each are unique, your response will be personal, neither right nor wrong. Welcome it as the beginning of a new day.

Even when you are ready to share your secret with a safe person, you may still feel your resistance. Often it is the fear of judgment, irrespective of the secret's intensity, that causes anxiety. Simply be present with whatever you're experiencing. If you can forgive yourself for whatever you think you did in the past, your self-judgment will likely dissolve. If you think your secret is unforgivable, open to the possibility that you did the best you could, given the resources you had back then. This so-called crime of yours is calling for acknowledgment, compassion, and empathy, as well as accountability. Consider that that particular event played a part in formulating your current value system, so vital to your well-being.

The Value of Sharing

The daunting task of revealing our secrets carries such positive, lasting benefits that the momentary fear will seem a small hurdle in hindsight. Embrace your fear and acknowledge it in your body from the Observer's point of view. Let go your judgment about fear and follow your breath where it takes you. As the Observer, you can follow the flow of your feelings and bring awareness and oxygen to the parts of your body that hold the block. Let yourself know that you are embracing your fear, that you are stretching yourself, allowing your humanness. Trust yourself.

When you share a secret, you are dropping your guard; and this is an invitation to your listener for a deeper connection. How will you choose whom to share your secret with? Be awake and discerning in that choice. You will set yourself up for failure if you choose someone who you sense is already judging you. Pick someone who you know is safe, who wants only the best for you.

When you share authentically what you have concealed for so long, you are, in essence, inviting the sun to shine in your darkest corner. It is an opportunity to get new information: to receive feedback and to do a reality check on the entire situation. You can have a new experience simply by revising an old one! And you get to choose how you interpret that experience, no matter what anyone else says about it. Even if the person you have chosen to reveal your secret to doesn't receive you, you can update your self-belief and bless yourself for having the courage to be transparent. The pay-off is in the act of sharing, not in the result.

Reconnect with Your Younger Self

Reconnecting with the younger self who constructed our secret, and being in relationship with that wounded part, is ultimately what we must do to forgive and accept ourself, and grow up. Spend some time with your wounded part. Go have a cup of tea or take a walk with the younger self who was involved in the event that gave rise to your secret. Be willing to get to know this aspect of yourself with compassion and ease. From a position of curiosity, from the Observer mode, ask this part of yourself any questions you may have, for example: *What were you feeling when you made that choice? What was going through your head?* Receive your younger self's answers warmly and gratefully.

Every new discovery about ourself makes us more complete, more human, and ultimately more at peace with ourself. When we act from a place of integrity—in alignment with the values of our ever-evolving integrated self—the world holds us with tender hands as we navigate toward our goals and our heart's desire. a secret, the impact of which we're

WORKBOOK: DAY 16

DATE: D / M / Y

Sharing Your Secret

How did you feel when you revealed your secret?

What were you convinced would happen? What actually happened?

How did you interpret your listener's reaction?

Integrating Your Secret

What does your younger self want you to know?

What does he/she need from you?

What kind of relationship are you committed to having with this wounded part of yourself?

How can your wounded part support you in moving toward your goals with more focus? What is its positive essence, and how can you use that essence today?

In what areas of your life will it serve you to add a conscious pinch of this positive essence?

DAY 17

YOUR ATTITUDE:
THE ART OF CHOOSING

Creating an intentional life means taking full responsibility for everything that goes on in your life and thereby navigating all circumstances from a place of choice. You identify yourself as a discerning adult empowered to choose, to cause your circumstances, rather than as the person your life is happening to, a life run by default, defined by seemingly accidental circumstances.

Our attitudes affect our outcomes, and most, if not all, lessons from the school of life can be mastered with an open, curious attitude. Conversely, we habitually "fail" at life when we dwell in the victim energy of resignation and pessimism. Many of us think that being an optimist or a pessimist is determined by some random gene. Life becomes a lot easier to navigate when we realize that optimism and pessimism are attitudes and therefore conscious choices.

How you choose to look at the world and all the circumstances in your life will impact your experience and therefore your results. Given that optimists have longer life spans, perform better in school and in their careers, and live happier and healthier lives than pessimists, what would you rather choose?

Some of us do not make the choice to be an optimist because we believe that optimists have to be happy all the time. We equate being optimistic with being cheerful and in a good mood. This is not true. An optimist invites all feelings while simultaneously maintaining an open and curious attitude.

Choose to Be an Optimist

Some of us think we have to wait for external situations to become positive before we can embrace a more optimistic view. Reverse that thinking process right now. Believe instead that if you have a lighter attitude, things will naturally improve right away. Believe in your own capacity to make the circumstances in your life go the way you want them to.

Positive thinking is a choice. For a start, you can watch your thoughts and only hold on to the ones that make you happier and more effective. You can practice this discipline from a place of intention in every area of your life. Optimism can be learned! It's an attitude, and you can consciously and spontaneously adjust your attitude anytime you like. If you are already an optimist, then you can even more consciously observe its powerful dynamics to further stretch the parameters of yourself.

Be Responsible for Your Choice: Success or Failure

Some of us choose to live our life as a pessimist because we have a notion that if we are prepared for the worst possible outcome, we will suffer less and handle rejection more easily. We think that forecasting the worst-case scenario will somehow protect us from the pain of failure. The problem with this kind of thinking, however, is that it actually perpetuates the experience of failure: we become a victim of our own attitude. By not imagining or expecting a positive result, we live in reaction to a fear of failure rather than in the expansive climate of possible success. When we program ourself to expect a life of disappointment and failure, it does not make being rejected or failing any easier. Yet, simply imagining that the most desired circumstances will occur at least creates an opening for such things to manifest in reality. When we program ourself for failure, we have nothing to anticipate—and worse, heaven forbid, no dreams to deeply yearn for.

When we become a victim of our pessimistic view of life, we also miss out on the freedom that comes from perceiving multiple outcomes, seeing opportunities everywhere, and mining our so-called failures for their lessons, important building blocks to our wisdom. So, while pessimists live in reaction to the worst that can happen, optimists believe that anything is possible and are willing to see the opportunity and unexpected value in any situation.

Your Beliefs Create Your Reality

Deeply rooted in our Western culture are the beliefs that suffering makes us noble, life has value only when we struggle, and being happy is hard work. The underlying belief is that nothing comes easy.

How many of these beliefs are you holding on to? Such beliefs compose a pessimistic view of life that accepts that suffering, struggle, hard work, and difficulties are facts of life. They unconsciously program you to swim against the current, against the natural flow of life. Catch yourself when you are holding on to these kinds of thoughts, and consciously choose to believe their opposite. What would change if you accepted that life is easy, that finding fulfilling work is effortless, that you are naturally creative, resourceful, and whole? What if your task is simply to find the flow in your life and swim with all the circumstances, knowing that everything will naturally come your way? You can program yourself to experience success by simply choosing beliefs that generate a positive attitude.

When you label a situation as a problem, it is the label itself that is the problem. Forward movement, produced by creativity and open-mindedness, requires flexibility and expansive perception. When you believe that something is a problem, you get stuck because your thinking becomes rigid and small, not conducive to your getting what you want. The optimist, on the other hand, looks at a potentially problematic situation and asks, *How can I dance with this? What am I going to do with this?* While the pessimist looks for whom to blame and who needs to change to better the situation, the optimist wonders what actions to take. Optimists determine their desired result, while pessimists hardly know what they want, only what they don't want. Optimists recognize that the perfect life still has glitches in it, while pessimists believe that one negates the other. The optimist accepts a difficult circumstance as a challenge and commits to resolving it with creativity and neutrality—no drama, no overreacting, no over personalizing, no spiraling to the bottom. The question "What can I learn from this?" always operates in the background.

You can program yourself to expect success. You can cultivate a positive attitude that will transform difficulties into opportunities. Optimism is a habit that can be learned. All you need to do is to authentically practice coming from a place of curiosity.

Practice Makes Perfect:
Guidelines for How to Practice Being an Optimist

- Ask the question "What can I learn from this?" rather than label a situation as a problem.
- Seek new angles from which to perceive a situation or to find a solution. Invite input and feedback.
- Be willing to update your belief system. Let go of the stories from the past that do not empower you.
- Perceive a win in every situation, whether or not you get what you want. When you don't get what you want, turn it into a winning situation by mining the treasure of the lesson available.

- Accept all difficult situations as challenges and solve them from a neutral place of non-attachment and trust.

- Be willing to renegotiate your movement step-by-step without overfocusing on the end result. Reassess frequently, through a wide-angle lens.

- Know your capabilities and take time off to recharge before you get overwhelmed.

- Be aware of your thoughts and notice where they lead you. Change any thought that doesn't serve you.

- Consider others and yourself equally. Generously express appreciation from a place of authentic gratitude—which is natural when you find value in everything.

- Find flow in adversity, in life's glitches, and trust that there is always a solution.

WORKBOOK: Day 17

Date: D / M / Y

Choosing to Be an Optimist

Study the guidelines for being an optimist. What can you add to the list?

-
-
-
-
-
-
-
-

Pick one guideline and apply it to an area of your life in which you experience struggle or suffering.

How does the optimist's lens alter your perspective on the situation?

In noticing your thoughts and how they define your attitude, are you generally an optimist or a pessimist?

Specify the areas of your life that are stagnating due to your pessimism. What successes toward your heart's desire can you foresee if you practice being an optimist in those areas?

Day 18

The Power of Your Thoughts: What You Focus On Grows

A mind closed off to the possibility that we are powerful beyond belief and can get all that we want is a mind that spends way too much time in pessimism. Our thoughts are very powerful: When we focus on scarcity or what we don't want, that's what we create; that's what grows. Likewise, when we focus on what we want, it grows. In essence, we create experiences and circumstances that confirm everything we believe. If you believe you will fail, you probably will. Conversely, if you believe you will succeed, your odds will increase considerably. Think of the process as a painting. If it were called "My Success," the colors, brushstrokes, and forms would be different than those of a painting called "My Failure." What you fill the blank canvas of your life with creates your reality, and a big component of that process is your thoughts. Once you recognize this correlation, it will be easier to adjust your thoughts so that they compose a picture of you successfully reaching your goals. You are the artist. The canvas is blank until you fill it.

Think Big and Go Home

Embracing the radical act of living your life intentionally, seeing the connections between your thinking and your results, is the fastest road to your destination. When you stop filtering your enthusiastic and Big thoughts, your life starts to flow in a fluid, effortless way. And when you believe in yourself and in what you want, take action with integrity, and hold yourself accountable to your thoughts and actions, it becomes easier and easier to succeed. Every chapter in this book has been designed toward that end. Are you willing to step up to the plate?

The War Against You

We use our own thinking process as a weapon against ourself. We do this constantly by spinning thoughts that make us doubt ourself, put ourself down, kill our confidence, and feed our negativity as if it were based in fact.

Notice the thoughts that pass through your head. When you embark on a new project, do you typically have thoughts like these? "This project is too big for me." "My goals are unrealistic." "What are the odds of that happening?" or "I'm never going to be able to pull this off." How do you treat yourself when the thought that you're not good enough comes up? What happens when the thought that your goals are too big for you arises? Most of us are stunned when we observe how we actually treat ourself inside our head.

Make a Peace Treaty with Yourself

Similar to your work on Days 4 and 8, ask yourself, *Who would I be without self-deprecating thoughts?* Most of my clients roar when they answer this question; they just can't hold back their enthusiasm. Allow yourself to experience the immediate freedom of not having those detrimental thoughts ruling your life.

Outlined below are four steps to powerful thinking. Read them with your Big open mind, and dance with the possibilities. If you are already doing these steps, good for you: you will get even more conscious of their application. If you are triggered by the suggestions posed below, good for you: you will get to push your comfort zone. If you lie somewhere between, good for you! Use it all to your advantage. Notice what you do already, notice what triggers you, keep working on yourself with compassion and empathy, and, as usual, practice, practice, practice.

The Four Steps to Powerful Thinking

As you move toward achieving your goals and your heart's desire, review these four steps whenever you feel stuck, discouraged, or resigned:

1. Stop blaming others or outside circumstances for what doesn't work in your life. Hold yourself Big by taking ownership of all that has happened and is happening in your life. Is it working for you to blame other people or circumstances? Be honest. Try on the possibility that you have played a part in all your disappointments and failures. Personal responsibility doesn't mean self-blame. Bring compassion to yourself, and trust that you are ready to shift to a new perspective.

2. Consciously claim your thoughts and revise them, as you've learned in this book, so that they support you in obtaining your desired results. Ask yourself these questions when you notice that your thought is destructive and full of blame and judgment:

    - How am I treating myself when I have this thought? How do I feel?
    - Who would I be without this thought?

    Notice the excitement that is generated when you are free of a negative thought.

3. Identify your bottom line, the scenario for the goal at hand that you are unwilling to go below. It is important to define its conditions, and don't dwell on them. Remember, you create what you focus on.

4. Define the best-case scenario, your desired results in all their delicious details, and linger there, enjoying what you truly want and imagining it grow. Your imagination is the fertilizer of your dreams.

WORKBOOK: DAY 18

DATE: D / M / Y

Creating Powerful Thinking

Pick one of your goals to work on during this exercise. Envision yourself with 100% belief in your capabilities.

What is the best-case scenario for this goal?

What is your non-negotiable bottom line, the marker you are not willing to go below?

Who do you need to be to get the results you want?

Why is it important that you get these results?

Who are you going to be when you achieve this goal?

Repeat this exercise with as many goals as you want.

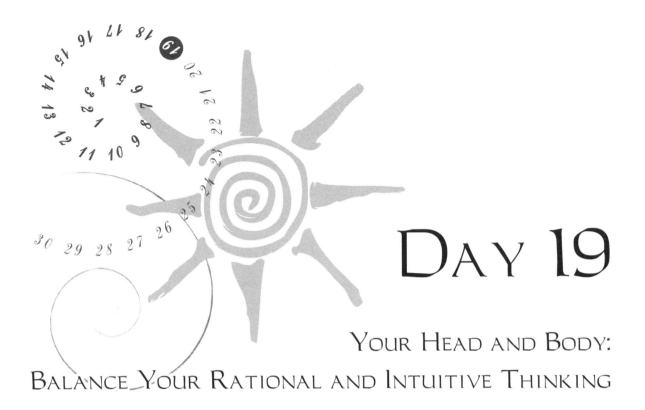

DAY 19

YOUR HEAD AND BODY: BALANCE YOUR RATIONAL AND INTUITIVE THINKING

A life lived consciously, with intention, is a life that values balance among its various aspects. It maintains balance between rational thinking and intuitive thinking, between doing and being, between the personal and the professional, and between work and play.

Rational thinking is the product of our practical mind; intuitive thinking is the product of our senses. A balance between them is essential because it integrates the intuitive wisdom of the body with the practical perception of the mind.

We in Western society make so many decisions based on our rational thinking. When we come from our head, we choose what makes sense within the parameters of our comfort zone, the tried and true, usually disregarding our intuition, which otherwise guides us to inexplicably pursue an unfamiliar path and act in unfamiliar ways. When we ignore our hunches and gut feelings, we often regret it later on.

While it's important to consider our decisions in our head, assessing available information in a linear way and reasoning out the best course of action, it is equally important to weigh in the information supplied by our intuition. In order to accurately comprehend an experience or issue, we need to listen to both: our head, with its rational perception, and our body, which holds our intuitive thinking.

Your Body: A Fantastic Tool

Most of us recognize the remarkable capacities of our mind; yet, as human beings, we are also equipped with a body that can support us in making decisions. The gut feelings, the butterflies we sometimes experience in our stomach, the physical pain or ailments—all are bodily expressions of our inner feelings. All are part of an information system designed to impart valuable knowledge about ourself to ourself. If we were to notice the body's operation in its fullest capacity, we would acknowledge that it is not only a container for all our feelings; it is also able to illuminate experiences and issues from an intuitive angle. We have all had the experience of meeting a person and instantly knowing we don't like him or her—it's not rational or explainable; it is simply a feeling. Some of us discount this information because it's not logical; yet, in not validating our body's signals, we deprive ourself of a well-rounded assessment of the person or situation.

Harmonizing our head reasoning and our body intuition, and making decisions from that balanced perspective, is an essential part of a life lived with clear intention. Often our head wants us to consider convenience, or what makes us look good. Shoulds or shouldn'ts inevitably factor in when we are considering options for action. Our body, however, can help us step out of our habitual thinking patterns and break new ground. When we honor our intuition and trust our hunches, we expand our comfort zone and live more fully in the present moment. Sometimes an intuitive leap of faith—which we can take because we have a fabulous parachute—is the absolutely perfect action, even if our rational mind is totally opposed.

Take Leaps of Faith from a Grounded Place

How do you take these kinds of chances? How do you recognize and interpret your body's signals and integrate them with your rational thoughts to make the decisions that are best for you? Easy! Be in the present, be in your body, and be clear about your intention. Being in the present means assessing a situation from a place of neutrality by forgetting about everything that went wrong in the past and letting go of the anticipation of future failures.

Balancing our rational and intuitive thinking requires the radical act of being in the present, of connecting with who we are in the now. We consult our rational head, we consult our body's hunches and sensations, and we blend them from the neutral perspective of our Observer. Grounded in the present moment, we trust our parachute, constantly adjusting our attitude, remaining curious about the situation and ourself. Open to dancing with adversity as a learning partner, we align our actions with our core values, moving with integrity toward our heart's desire.

A Healthy Mind in a Healthy Body

When we treat our body with respect, nourishing and caring for it on the physical level, it repays us tenfold with clear, helpful information, which we can access at any time. Anytime we need to know something, we can tune in to our body, sinking into our rich and cavernous belly to find answers buried in our profound inherent knowledge.

Mens sana in corpore sano is Latin for "a healthy mind in a healthy body." When you honor this philosophy with consistent actions, you can have it all. With your mind and body aligned, you can focus on what you want to grow, trust that you are in the right place, and listen to your mind-body wisdom with the confidence that there is buried treasure in everything. This is a life of balance.

Intend to Create Balance

When we are not willing to embrace that both rational and intuitive thinking are integral components of our decision-making process rather than polarities, we can become stuck or hindered in our forward movement because we rely on only one or the other source of information. If we are attached to either right or wrong, good or bad, intellectual or creative, rational or intuitive, we are out of balance. Balance comes when we utilize all our faculties, even if they initially seem incongruous. Using your intuitive thinking in conjunction with your rational thinking opens you up to a wider range of possibilities. You will get better results, no matter what your goal, for the simple reason that you are fully employing all your resources at a deeper level.

To stretch your comfort zone and create balance between the two modes of thinking, commit to having an experience that is unfamiliar to you. Are you more of a rational thinker? Push your edge by honoring your intuition. Are you more of an intuitive thinker? Push your edge by listening to your rational thoughts. In either case, trust that you will know how to do it, and rely on your inner sense of balance to find its perfect pivot point between your rational mind and your intuitive body. You might lose your balance a few times, yet any accidental falls will be cushioned by your innate desire to become a well-rounded human being, living an intentional life of full-out expression.

WORKBOOK: DAY 19

DATE: D / M / Y

Balancing Your Rational and Intuitive Thinking

What areas of your life would benefit from a more rational approach?

What areas of your life would benefit from your being guided more by your intuition?

How do you know when you are in balance, in the perfect pivot point between your rational mind and your intuitive body?

Considering this perfect pivot point and your goals that have been primarily directed by either your rational mind or your intuition, what changes can you make in how you've been pursuing your goals?

Day 20

Sole Focus:
One Thing at a Time—Easy Does It!

Relationship and deep connection with others is one of the most basic and vital concepts to master in order to live a balanced life. Many of us in Western culture still measure our success by what we do, rather than by who we are in the pursuit and accomplishment of our goals and in our interactions with others. Our society is constructed by the ways we relate and communicate with each other and express who we are and what we want. To effectively communicate in any medium, and to express our own unique vision in everything we do, we need to be present.

To be present, to be in the moment, and to thereby be able to express ourself clearly and receive others with the same clarity, requires a single-minded focus. If you do not acknowledge the importance of relationships with others in your life and honor them with the sole attention they deserve, you may be sacrificing deep connections in favor of busy-ness.

When you focus on one thing at a time, you are clear, centered, and concise; and you can move through tasks and communications with profound authenticity and effectiveness. As a result, people receive you loud and clear. They perceive you as a dependable individual, and you are better able, then, to build a foundation of trust for your personal interactions. People like to be received when they express themselves, and they will feel more received after a two-minute conversation if you are present, than after talking to you for hours if you are multitasking. The amount of time you spend with someone is not what is important; your state of mind is. When you are singularly focused and in the present, it's a win-win situation, resulting in deeper intimacy with everyone in your life, from your closest family members to your business associates.

Slow Down to Get More Done

When you slow down and focus on one thing at a time, not only will people relate to you better, you will actually save more time. When you multitask, inevitably something isn't done right and often needs to be repeated. For instance, if you have ever tried to write an e-mail while talking on the phone, either you missed half the conversation or your e-mail was a grammatical nightmare. You had to ask the person on the end of the line to repeat what they had said, or you had to clarify your e-mail when the recipient let you know that they didn't quite understand what you had written. Not only is it inefficient, the people you are relating to are left feeling invalidated and confused.

Multitasking is a surefire way to not be present to multiple things at the same time. It's literally a waste of time and energy and a behavioral pattern that is grossly overrated in today's world. It results in miscommunications and poor personal connections, which cause confusion and frustration. Our colleagues do not accurately receive us when we communicate while multitasking; our spouses and children don't respond to our requests when we are shouting orders while running out of the house, doing sixteen other things. If you are always complaining that there isn't enough time in the day, always out of breath and running on to the next thing to do, it is only a matter of time before your personal and professional relationships pay the price.

Being present to the interaction itself between you and another, with your mind focused exclusively on that task, will facilitate clear communication and closer human dynamics. Try it. Try it with your children, your intimate partner, your business associate. Slow down, keep your sentences simple, with clear intent, and listen for the response. If you are not received or understood, try again. You will be surprised by the results, how much time you save, and the ease with which your relationships unfold. Slowing down is the best way to get more done!

Do One Thing at a Time (Always)

You will obtain equally valuable results when you apply the do-one-thing-at-a-time concept to everything. When you are present and focused on one thing at a time, whatever that is, your time will seem to stretch and the results will be infinitely more rewarding.

Though I don't typically share my life as an example of the concepts I present, I would like to make an exception here. I have personally experienced everything that I have suggested to my clients, and focusing on one thing at a time is the concept that has most impacted my life. People often comment on how many things I am able to successfully accomplish in a very short time. My life is very full—I write books, run a business, have fulfilling hobbies, meditate, exercise—and people assume that the only way one can accomplish so much is to multitask. Let me be clear: I do not multitask. And it is because I don't multitask that I am extremely focused and get it all done. I live my life with intentional passion, honoring what I do and surrendering control, knowing that *life is never done*—and choosing to do one thing at a time. Always.

I have become very good at saying no when I know that taking on one more thing will throw me off balance and weaken my focus. I do not spend time with friends if I cannot be present to our interaction. I would rather spend infrequent quality time with my friends, when I can be fully present, than say yes to too many people, resulting in poor communication and diluted connections. We think that if we don't say yes to everyone, we are being rude. To the contrary, if you are saying yes simply to be polite, when you already have too much on your plate, people will feel your half-heartedness and frenetic energy and be impacted negatively.

Life Is Never Done

There are twenty-four hours in a day. That is a fact. If the tasks and chores you have planned for the day add up to forty-eight hours of activity, chances are in trying to do them all, you will do them poorly. You will not be received as effectively, people may actually resent you, you will feel like a basket case, and, most counterproductive of all, what you were rushing to do will likely have to be redone. Your next day will begin with a sense of anxiety, of incompletion, as if you have run out of breath.

What would your life be like if you came to terms with the reality that life is never done? You can kill yourself trying to do everything on your to-do list today, yet tomorrow there will be more phone calls to return, more tasks to perform, more chores to do. What would your life be like if you focused on the present moment only, did one thing at a time, nurtured your personal relationships by giving them your undivided attention?

Life is never done. Learn how to prioritize and to delegate; be willing to give up power and control for sanity and deeper connections. There is only one of you, and you are responsible for that you. Remember *mens sana in corpore sano?* When you need to be in ten places at once, choose to focus on what best serves you and your heart's desire.

Swim with the Current

Do a quick inventory of what you need to do to be centered and focused. When we take ten to thirty minutes during our day to consciously recharge, the results are incredible. We can relax, ease into our tasks, and experience the execution of those tasks in a much smoother fashion.

Life is easy if you can just accept that it is, the way a fish accepts the current and swims with it. We are conditioned to make it complicated, to want more, to be perpetually unhappy and unsatisfied, caught up in the doing-doing-doing of life and the pursuit of unobtainable goals. Rather than go with the flow, accepting ourself as the powerful and magnificent individual that we are, we make ourself struggle. Commit to making your life easy. Prioritize, delegate, slow down, and flow with the current of life and human connection. Switch your frame of mind to the concept "life is easy," and that is how you will experience it. You can do it; you are powerful beyond measure.

WORKBOOK: Day 20

DATE: D / M / Y

Doing One Thing at a Time

Pick one of your relationships and commit to having, for one full day, the experience of being present to every interaction with that person. Afterward, record how those interactions differed from your usual experience of that relationship.

Choose one day when you will intend to not multitask, when you will consciously do one thing at a time. Afterward, record how that day differed from your typical day.

Day 21

Being and Doing: Who You Are and What You Do

Often we focus so exclusively on our goals, zooming in to the final result, that our sole journey is one of doing. Embracing the perspective of the Observer gives you the capacity to shift from the laser-pointer-lens view to the grand-angle-lens view, offering a comprehensive vision that includes you, the journey, and the goals. When you visualize yourself as the Observer, surveying the whole scene from the top of the metaphorical lighthouse, the resultant 360-degree view takes account of your past, present, and future.

This wider angle—the one that includes you in the picture—expands your focus from what you are doing to who you are being while you are doing. This shift of consciousness to who you are being while pursuing your goals is important because you will reach your goals faster if you are happy while you are getting there. Finding out who you are in the present is what you have been investing your time and energy in for the past twenty days. Every day of this manual is designed to give you a deeper self-knowledge and thereby broaden your grand-angle view, creating more balance between doing and being. In a world that overrates doing-doing-doing, you can actually choose to go against the tide and consciously prioritize who you are over what you do.

Embrace Another Perspective

Our doing-doing-doing attitude usually stems from the endless lists we impose on ourself. There is a difference between doing it all and being efficient. What would it be like to embrace the perspective that life is never done, to be unwilling to drain your resources in order to arrive at some future life, in favor of fully experiencing your life *while* you accomplish your tasks?

It's called prioritizing. Don't laugh! Yes, I know you know how to prioritize, though you likely know from a place of *doing*. I would like you to consider prioritizing from a place of *being*. How can you *be* a prioritizer? Being a prioritizer means being a discerning adult who knows that:

- Life is never done; you can return all your phone calls and e-mails, and tomorrow there will be more.
- There is only one of you, so you ask yourself on an ongoing basis what is most crucial for you to invest your time and expertise in, given that there are twenty-four hours in day.
- Being fulfilled while living your life is non-negotiable.
- Connection with people requires a sole focus.
- Choices and their potential outcomes are best assessed with a grand-angle lens.

Take a Deep Breath

You may be so caught in the doing that you forget to acknowledge all the results, big and small, moving from task to task and adding more to your to-do list. One way you can reduce stress and put consciousness into your day is to take a deep breath after you have completed a task on your list. By stopping and acknowledging yourself at each small milestone, you are "smelling the roses" and taking time to *be* a human *being*. Take a deep breath, make yourself a cup of tea, walk to a window, and look outside: the open view, this conscious stopping to recharge, will support you in shifting to *being* a prioritizer.

We say we are busy; we say we have no time: we can't squeeze into our day one more thing. True or false? False. If we had a terminal illness, we would find the time to have treatments and survive. We would prioritize the treatments. Being a conscious human being means being able to find solutions and implement positive changes in our life before a life-threatening illness forces us to prioritize our well-being to the top of the list.

When your list of things to do rules your life, when your interactions with your loved ones are frantic, when you don't eat properly, when you forget how to be, how to embrace your humanness, you are doing a great disservice to yourself, and you are modeling a life-threatening lifestyle to the people around you.

Create the Openness for New Things to Come to You

The biggest value of all in living life as a human *being* is that you are creating the opportunity for new people and new circumstances to come to you because you are being open. When you are trapped in the doing, many options and solutions to your issues might be right in front of you, yet you are too busy to see them.

I had a client who was so busy in the doing of everything that she became very stressed and was diagnosed with life-threatening high blood pressure. She resolved to be more relaxed, and she focused exclusively on that goal. To her already busy schedule, she added a daily yoga class and twice-daily meditation because those were the *things to do* if one wanted to relax. Omitting herself in the process, she disregarded the fact that her schedule was already overbooked and that she hated both yoga and meditation. I am sure I don't need to tell you that the result was horrible. It wasn't until she was rushed to the hospital emergency room that she got the message.

She thought her choice was between doing and being, and because she was terrified to leave her *doing* comfort zone, she never saw the option of creating balance between the two until the choice became life or death. Often we don't realize that the key in life is to find the balance that works for us, the balance that will stretch us out of our comfort zone and open doors to new discoveries, new attitudes, new perspectives. We get trapped in a modus operandi and thus keep doing more and more of the same limiting behaviors. One cannot find solutions to an issue with the same consciousness that created the issue.

My client had done everything in order to live a privileged life; she worked hard and created a very successful business. Now, at this point in her life, she was caught in the doing for the sake of it, until her own body disrupted her doing-doing-doing status quo by collapsing and thereby forcing her to make drastic life changes. Then is when she made the choice to bring more balance into her life, to experience her life from a place of being. Opening up to my coaching, she wanted to learn how to listen to herself, to find a meditation practice that suited her, to exercise according to her body's wants, and to fully embrace her new life and softer perspective of the world. She chose herself coming from a *being* essence. She brought that *being* into her work and was able to continue her success from a place of awareness and newfound respect for her human needs.

Her recovery was short of miraculous. Her new life perspective allowed her to see herself from a place of stillness, and in that place, she was able to embrace who she was and who she had become, including all her achievements and shortcomings. She got the chance to live the later part of her life experiencing a broader, more enriching viewpoint.

In my practice as a coach, I work to support people in pushing their comfort zone and experiencing themselves from multiple perspectives. Most important, I support them in moving from a state of endless doing to one of being while they're doing, and in finding balance between the two.

Values Overlap

We know that, in life, practice makes perfect, and we are willing to apply this concept to most anything we want to improve. A painter becomes a better painter by painting more; an athlete become a better athlete by exercising more; a lawyer becomes a better lawyer by taking on more cases.

Generally speaking, when we want to improve at something, we become aware of our capacities, try a few things, decide what works and what doesn't, and then simply move forward. Often, however, we are not willing to apply the same determination to shifting from patterns that don't work for us, to patterns that might suit us better. Though we may devote hours at the gym to improve our endurance on the treadmill, we are reluctant to invest our efforts in finding ways to relax, to be nice to ourself, to push our comfort zone. My aforementioned client became a very successful businesswoman by passionately applying herself to perfect a method in her job. She was willing to be flexible, to persevere with what worked, and to drop what didn't work. She had fun; she could connect with her own successful-at-business persona; she could be who she needed to be to shine at her work. In her personal life, however, namely with respect to her health, she couldn't duplicate that winning formula. When it comes to ourself and our emotional, spiritual, and metaphysical development, we often think we need to know it all, so we capitulate to old patterns and unsuccessful modi operandi. We are not willing to observe what works and what doesn't and then choose how to continue. We keep our work life and inner self separate, shunning the understanding that the values that drive us overlap in all aspects of life and that it is our *being* human that needs more reward.

Shift from Doing to Being

If you want to shift to a more grounded place of being, from a place of doing, simply slow down in the moment and mindfully connect with your body during each breath. Let go of the frantic clutter of your rational brain and commit to experience life coming from your body as well as your head.

There are many tools available—tapes, books, exercises—to support you in sustaining your shift from doing to being. Most important in your practice is your intention to add more depth and serenity to your life, and to connect with your body. Being is a state of mind that requires your awareness to distinguish it from the doing state of mind. Once you have made this distinction, you can choose to practice being versus doing, and you can easily apply it to all areas of your life.

Practice, Practice, Practice

As they say, *Rome wasn't built in a day*. It takes only a moment to wake up to the awareness that our own formula hasn't been working, and only another moment to make the conscious choice to change. To build the new you, allow it to take as long as it takes, and have fun while you are practicing living a life of intention. Remember, *be* your life; don't *do* your life.

The best way to learn how to *be* is to choose a substantial block of time a day for you to practice how to *be*. That means you lie or sit on the couch, on your bed, outside, for a minimum of two hours a day* and just...*be*. You don't read, you don't meditate, you don't watch TV, listen to the radio, talk on the phone, use your computer, and you don't think. If creative thoughts flow in your head, let them roll where they go; if you have *doing* thoughts, gently push them away. Yes, you know the difference between *being* and *doing* thoughts. If it helps you relax, you can

---

*The key in determining how long to practice being is to stretch yourself: you want to commit to an amount of time that is edgy for you. Obviously, if you have young kids, you will have to coordinate with someone else, in which case even half an hour may be a stretch. In other words, choose a time that elicits this response: "What?! That long? I could never do that!" When a spiritual teacher of mine prescribed three hours of being a day for three months, I thought there was no way in hell I would be able to do it...and yet, wow! Now I can do a whole day of being.

imagine situations that have invited feelings of happiness and fulfillment. For example, imagine a walk in the forest with your dog, a fun childhood experience, a moment when you were totally content.

At the beginning, you might condition yourself to think this is hard, maybe even impossible. Let go of that thought. We were born as human *beings*: a state of *being* is actually our original nature. If you practice this exercise regularly, every day for at least three months, you will let go of the frantic energy, focus on priorities a lot better, have more clarity, communicate more easily with people and be received at a deeper level, talk and do less and accomplish more, and model to your loved ones that you can take care of yourself and allow them to *be* as well. Being will become such a natural state for you—again—that when you run into a doing-doing-doing person, their frenetic energy and talk will initially be jarring, and probably annoying. This will be a great opportunity to witness through the Observer's eye, to not judge the other person and to acknowledge yourself for your forward movement.

As I'd said earlier, if you want to improve at something, you become aware of your capacities, try a few things, decide what works and what doesn't, and then practice it to gain the experience to perfect it. If you want to excel, if you want fulfillment in your life, however, then you shift into the state of *being*, connecting with your inner essence and transcending to a place of Bigness, where your Big Picture is the focus. You *be* you.

WORKBOOK: Day 21

Date: D / M / Y

Becoming Aware of Who You Are Being

Review your goals, including all the steps. With the Observer's lens, expand the view to include you.

Who would you like to be while accomplishing your goals? Record as many adjectives as you like, stringing them together with "and." You are a multifaceted human being; you can hold as many attributes as you want: fun <u>and</u> integrated <u>and</u> considerate <u>and</u> committed to your health <u>and</u> relaxed <u>and</u> trusty <u>and</u>...

Shifting from a Human Doing to a Human Being

Think about your life right now and consciously observe the areas in which you are a human doing. How would shifting to a place of being work better for you?

How can you slow down and connect to your body to make that shift?

DAY 22

THE ZONE!
DANCE WITH YOUR RESOURCES

"The zone" is that place of synchronicity where everything is aligned with perfect timing, where decisions are easy to make and you experience excitement and happiness. The zone is the place that exists between a second ago and a second from now, where you are in the present and able to access your creativity. In this place, you find the inner tools that support you to easily move forward with flow, balance, purpose, and grounded enthusiasm.

When a challenge presents itself in your life and you label it a "problem," that label itself is the problem. Calling something a problem is what limits you, not the issue itself. Once you define something as a problem, you leave the zone, your most creative place from which to resolve issues; you go into your head, and your negative thoughts get the best of you. Living in your head is fine for linear thinking and looking at details, yet not at all conducive for flexible, intuitive, and creative thinking.

The zone is where your feeling body is able to bring you information that broadens your frame of mind and opens you to solutions. As long as you have stamped something a problem, you are not in the right frame of mind to ever solve it because you have locked yourself out of the zone and the resources available there. Problems—or what you label as such—are, by their very nature, unnecessary obstacles. Actually, that is the meaning of the word "problem." The word "problem" comes from the Greek noun **πρόβλημα**, which means "obstacle," and from the verb **προβαλλω**, which literally means "to put an obstacle in front."

Witness the Power of Language

The impact of language on your resourcefulness can be experienced immediately. Try it right now. Label your biggest issue a "problem." Say it out loud: "My problem is _____ ."

What happens to you? Most likely you feel as though an insurmountable weight has landed on your shoulders, and possibly your chest has become constricted. Perhaps even your body posture has sunk, a physical expression of your deflated attitude. People who walk around with problems to solve are people who tend to collapse in desperation and, in their despondency, grasp at anything as a solution.

Now go back to where you were before you labeled your issue as a problem. Think about the same issue. Take a deep breath, sink into your belly, and ask yourself, *How can I dance with this? What is a creative way of looking at this issue?*

People who look at issues with this attitude usually have an uplifted posture. They walk around with a bounce in their step; they are curious, positive, and interested in opening to solutions. They are able to discern the best resolution by accessing their creativity and reframing their issue as an exciting challenge. There is no drama in this place; there is, instead, effective thinking and brainstorming. I am sure you were able to instantly feel and experience the difference between the two attitudes. It can really be just that easy.

Issues are issues. You focus on them; you are willing to dance with them; you find a solution; you move on. Problems are unsolvable. They cause drama; they spin you around with negative thoughts and criticism. The thoughts generated when you label an issue as a problem are like quicksand: you seldom get out alive because you're grabbing at solutions out of a sense of desperation rather than weighing possible solutions and resolving by choice.

When You Are Not in the Zone

Many people believe in Murphy's Law, that anything that can go wrong *will* go wrong. In the zone, it is the opposite: there is an abundance of synchronicity, and what can go right *does* go right. How do you learn to identify when you are in the zone? By first identifying when you are *not*—and making adjustments to your attitude as soon as you notice. You are out of the zone when:

- Issues become problems.
- Your creativity, imagination, and intuition are dead.
- Limiting thoughts arise: you focus on past failures or forecast future disappointments.
- You feel needy.
- You feel powerless, overwhelmed, and frantic.
- You experience fear and chronic worry.
- You have a negative mindset: no solution is quite right.
- You exhibit either/or thinking.
- You experience a state of anxiety and struggle.
- You can't discern any choices.
- You are closed to your greatness.
- You are deeply critical of yourself and others.
- You feel stuck and impatient.

Into the Zone!

When an issue arises, you can choose to step into the zone, just as John Travolta's character, Tony Manero, does in the movie *Staying Alive*. You can leap into a rhythmic synchronicity deep in your body and, taking a big breath, dance yourself out of your issues! To intentionally access the zone, discover your proactive stance that says, "I am here and I got it!" Being in the zone is a conscious choice! You are in the zone when:

- Issues become opportunities.
- Your creativity, imagination, and intuition are thriving.
- Your thoughts are expansive and in the present moment.
- You are in touch with what you want.
- You feel powerful, centered, and calm.
- You feel trusting and relaxed.
- You experience confidence.
- You have a solution-focused mindset: anything is possible.
- You experience a state of flow and ease.
- You perceive infinite choices.
- You are in tune with your spirituality.
- You are deeply grateful.
- You feel inspired and patient.

The Power of LSD: Laugh, Sing, and Dance

The quickest way to access the zone is LSD: laugh, sing, and dance. You can do this with ease. You can put on your favorite music and dance, sing your favorite song at the top of your lungs, or fake laughing until it becomes a natural belly laugh. There are many other immediate ways to get into the zone, and you can invite your creativity to come up with the one that works best for you. It can be as simple as taking a few very deep breaths and sinking into your body. You can walk to a window and look outside to change your perspective. All these ways can be used individually or in conjunction with each other, and they will transform any overwhelming or limiting state into a place of creativity and vibrant intention.

Take a few moments to experiment and discover what method is the most effective for you to access the zone, and then practice, practice, practice. Practice makes perfect: the more you step into the zone, the easier it will be for you to spend more and more time there, until one day you will not even notice the transition. You will be there all the time.

Living a life of conscious intention is easier than you might think. If you are simply willing to discover what will make you happy and to practice that, it will become part of your modus operandi. There is no big secret to being fulfilled: do the things that make you happy, rather than repeat your painful mistakes over and over, hoping for a different outcome.

Learn to intentionally walk your talk; it is the most effectual means toward living a truly fulfilled life. You will more easily achieve your goals and experience your heart's desire. Why make things more complicated than they are? Stop struggling and surrender to the simplicity that *life is easy*.

Easy Does It

If you have enrolled in the school of hard knocks, or have sentenced yourself to the belief that life is hard, that life is a struggle, STOP THAT RIGHT NOW! Instead, remember what *easy* feels like, and imprint in your brain what it feels like when you are in the zone.

WORKBOOK: Day 22

Date: D / M / Y

Take It Easy...

No workbook exercises today ~ go dance and step into the zone with consciousness—and have fun!

DAY 23

OXYGEN MASK:
TAKE CARE OF YOURSELF FIRST

Sometimes we have conflicting values. When I coach clients on the issue of releasing stress from their life and the importance of aligning actions with values, I often notice conflicting values that they may not be aware of. Having conflicting values creates stress and doesn't allow us to move forward out of a clear choice.

Many of us value professional success, an exciting personal life, participation in the community, our parental involvement, and a healthy lifestyle, among many other values. In our competitive world, we are pushed almost to a breaking point to live to satisfy our boss, our partner, and our own expectations. Juggling has become a necessity; multitasking has proven to be inefficient. Everything takes time, and it doesn't seem to matter how little sleep we need and how good we are at rushing around; there are still only twenty-four hours in every day to handle all the details of our contemporary life.

The metaphor I use the most in my coaching practice is that of the oxygen mask used by airlines. Flight attendants instruct passengers to first put one over their own mouth before helping others, in the event that oxygen masks are released during an emergency. This same lesson applies once we step off the plane: we must take care of ourself before we can take care of others.

When you are feeling pressure from multiple sources, and you are conflicted about whether to work late, go to the gym, or go to a City Hall meeting that will decide the future of your neighborhood, put your well-being first. Make yourself your priority. Can you reasonably finish an important project by working overtime another night, have a good workout, and be a supporter of your community? Assess which one of your activities will give you the oxygen you need to maintain your overall excellence in the long term.

Today's world often provides us with too many choices, and that in itself can cause us stress. Doing too much and our drive for perfection can put us over the edge, and then we risk jeopardizing it all. Spending an hour with a pal, having a few good laughs, might be the oxygen you need to complete your project at work the following morning. Wearing your oxygen mask with intention and taking the Observer's wide-angle perspective will support you in making choices in the moment that are appropriate for long-range success.

It may be that choosing to juggle working late, doing your workout, and attending the community meeting serves you in the long run. You may consciously choose to renegotiate a deadline in favor of not giving up a family event, or to give up the meeting at City Hall for a few extra hours of sleep. Whatever action you choose, whatever value you decide to prioritize, as long as you do it with awareness, it will be appropriate, and it will serve your life direction.

To choose the actions that best meet your conflicting values, remember these behaviors: make yourself your number-one priority, and wear your oxygen mask before trying to help others. Put yourself in the present, in the *being* mode, and ask yourself, the discerning adult, what is the most important choice for you in this moment. Ask yourself if you would benefit more from just *being* than from any of the *doing* options before you. Then take a deep breath into your oxygen mask and enjoy the experience of your choice.

WORKBOOK: Day 23

Date: D / M / Y

Identifying Your Oxygen

What is the oxygen you choose to breathe to keep yourself balanced or to fortify yourself when you feel stressed and troubled?

What structure or sign can you set up for yourself, or with a friend, that lets you know it's time for you to wear your oxygen mask? For example, I have set up with a friend that if I say I can't breathe, it usually signals that my physical pain is becoming unbearable, and I need either an adjustment, a massage, or medication.

DAY 24

GRATITUDE:
STOP AND SMELL THE ROSES

Gratitude is part of a natural evolution. When we truly embrace the concept that there is treasure in everything, when we fully trust ourself to always be at the right place at the right time, and when we accept that only we are in charge of our life, being grateful in all circumstances and to everyone, including ourself, is easy. Whether you are a natural optimist or have intentionally set your course toward becoming one, you have probably noticed that people with an optimistic attitude are spontaneously appreciative and grateful. Optimists focus on their Big Picture, treasuring everything and everyone, no matter the initial appearance or impression.

When we stop taking things personally and are able to stand in the neutral place of the Observer, grounded and strong even in the eye of the storm, we are able to let go of our victimization and pessimistic outlook. Our world opens up, and we can taste the variety of riches now available to us. Once you are able to monitor your thinking process and choose what to do with the thoughts that don't support you, the world truly becomes a magical place where everything is possible and there is always a reason to celebrate.

Gratitude is not only an attitude, it is a stance, a way of being and thinking that requires some practice. A metaphor for gratitude is the old proverb "Stop and smell the roses." When we slow down, we are able to take the time to appreciate who and what is on our path and also ourself for who we are and what we do. What if, instead of forgetting to "smell the roses" in our busy plan to get somewhere, we made it a priority on our journey of life to move at a pace whereby details—the smell of roses—can be appreciated?

When we hold on to the past or become preoccupied with the future, we are not living in the present and therefore are unable to fully witness ourself and our life. We take our experiences for granted, and life feels dull and habitual. To fully experience gratitude, we must be present to the moment at hand. Feeling gratitude revitalizes our life by broadening our perception to include the wide lens of appreciation.

Practice Makes Perfect

Learn the good habit of slowing down regularly, and express gratitude and appreciation as a conscious practice until it becomes a natural way of living. By this point in your unique curriculum, you can acknowledge that relationship is one of the most enriching vehicles for personal growth. Taking the time to let people know how much you value them for who they are or for what they have done for you has great rewards. It opens your heart and theirs, deepening your connections, which, no doubt, has a ripple effect.

Make the decision that being grateful and appreciative will improve your life, and design a ritual, a precise, regularly repeated structure, to support you to slow down and smell the roses. Every Friday, for example, you might take a few minutes to sum up the week: What worked for you and what didn't? What do you want to carry over to next week? What do you need to complete? You might want to buy flowers on the way home to celebrate yourself and the end of another week and to symbolically shift to the weekend coming up and your time off. What plans have you made to recharge and to honor yourself and your loved ones? By assessing the week, consciously acknowledging both the events that went well and those that were more challenging and then letting them go, you energetically become better prepared for the week to come. Reaching out weekly to the people who have supported you—family, friends, and colleagues—to let them know how important their presence has been in your world will expand your experience of your life both in the moment and beyond, because you will attract more to be grateful for (what you focus on grows!).

Your Design, Your Way

If my suggestion to slow down on Fridays and assess your week as well as strategize for the next week has sent you into a panic because your Fridays are already nightmarishly busy, just stop—and redesign. Focus on one thing at a time, beginning with which of the week's seven days best suits your practice to slow down, assess the week, and express your gratitude and appreciation. If you already have a ritual in place, ask yourself if it is working: *Does my practice slow me down? Does it make me present to the fullness of my life? Does it support me in completing the past and creating my desired future?* You know by now how to stretch beyond your comfort zone and resistance. Don't let momentary discomfort stop you from redesigning the personalized systems you use to inventory your life.

I have a client who has designed a day for herself she calls Office Monday. On Monday mornings, she takes the first two hours after arriving to ground herself for the week. She buys herself flowers to symbolize her gratitude toward herself for creating this space to center and strategize. Her clients know that she is not available until late morning and that her time is sacred to her. She strategically plans every day of the week ahead and focuses herself into a work mode. She acknowledges her progress and explores what needs to be improved. Because this is also her time to clear and complete all the unfinished business from the previous week, she consciously keeps a lighter schedule on Mondays so that she has the flexibility to tie up any loose ends.

I have supported many people in designing their lives using their own formula, and so far, everyone agrees that expressing gratitude and appreciation—toward life, people, and themselves—has been a tremendous tool of growth and enrichment. My suggestion to create a ritual, an individualized practice that keeps you on track with a particular intention, has also been very well received and has produced excellent results for the people committed enough to try it.

Remember that your life is run by *you*, not by other people, not by your circumstances. Trust that you are the perfect designer of your practice for expressing gratitude for your unique life. Simply pick one day of the week and invite yourself into an experience of slow, deep noticing, allowing the flowers you purchase to open you to thankfulness. Let your gratitude grow, and extend it to those in your life. It will circle back, lavishing you with authentic appreciation for the magnificent person that you are. other values. In our competitive world, we are pushed almost to a breaking point to live to satisfy our boss, our partner, and our own expectations. Juggling has become a necessity; multitasking has proven to be inefficient. Everything takes time, and it doesn't seem to matter how little sleep we need and how good we are at rushing around; there are still only twenty-four hours in every day to handle all the details of our contemporary life.

WORKBOOK: Day 24

Date: D / M / Y

Designing Your Gratitude Ritual

Stop and smell the roses. Slow down, breathe deep, and open yourself to receive your inner guidance.

What day of the week do you dedicate to assessing your past week and creating the next one?

Day of the Week:

What would you like to do during that day regarding your...

- *...past week?*

- *...future week?*

Design your ritual that symbolizes this day as one of taking stock of what has gone before and assessing what is to come.

What do you appreciate about yourself and others? What are you grateful for in your life?

DAY 25

HARMONY:
HARMONIZE WITH YOURSELF AND
THE WORLD WILL HARMONIZE WITH YOU

Life is easy, and it flows when we are in harmony with ourself, with our values and our beliefs. When there is inner harmony among all aspects of ourself, the outside world will mirror that same state back to us in our external circumstances. When we consciously live our ideal life and do what we love doing, following the higher purpose of our existence, everything aligns in harmonic synchronicity.

Here is the catch: to be in harmony with ourself, we have to surrender to all that we are. We have to let go of self-judgment and the stereotypical notion that some qualities are good and some qualities are bad. What if we instead embraced the counterintuitive belief that our human imperfections are actually what make us perfect? When we embrace not only the light side, but also our dark side as a completion of our whole self, we invite inner harmony. If we do not accept all our polarities, the inevitable result is conflict both within ourself and with our world.

What a wild concept! To be in harmony with ourself, we have to know and accept the parts of ourself that we hate. Who would have guessed? The more we run away from all those parts, the more those disliked parts of our personality own us and rule us. The process of acceptance is called integration and results in inner and outer harmony. If we can accept who we are fully within our own self, then there is only harmony.

How do we integrate the so-called dark-side aspects of ourself? I define them here so that you can first assess which ones of your own you might still be resisting. Our dark-side qualities are those that are not accepted by society because they are considered, unjustly, bad qualities to have—for example, our judging nature, bitchiness, arrogance, bossiness, chauvinism, and egocentrism. Conditioned by the common belief that only light-side aspects are acceptable—qualities like niceness, generosity, and caring—we negate half of our true being.

If we let go of self-judgment and simply notice that we are both of the polarities that compose the whole picture, we will be more accepting of ourself and others, and life will be a lot easier. Without the dark, we cannot define light. Without greed, we cannot define generosity. We cannot be profoundly happy if we don't experience profound unhappiness. We cannot know altruism if we cannot love our selfish nature.

Embracing polarities also creates the nuances of feeling between the two extremes. If there were only white, with no contrasting black, there wouldn't be all the shades of gray in between. If there were only "amazing" with no "horrible" at the other end, you would never know the soft gentleness of "nice" in between the two. Integrating all parts of ourself means we can expand to include all the shades in between. We can accept good and bad, loving and hateful, graceful and clumsy, and everything in between. We can transcend an attachment to perfection and express the diversity that is our birthright as a human being. Extending the work we did on

Day 11, today we will work toward integrating our "negative" attributes in their entirety.

Mirror, Mirror on the Wall...

What we don't like in others is what we don't like in ourself. It's that mirror concept again—a great tool to learn to use. Everything that shows up in our external world is a reflection of who we are and what we need to integrate; our being triggered is the fastest way to access our internal discord and then choose to shift. Every time we are triggered by someone else's attitude is an opportunity to integrate that part within ourself. Accept this as a given truth; stop fighting it!

If you are not in tune with a part of yourself that irritates you in others, then you are not in harmony with yourself and, consequently, the world. Once you accept that quality as a part of your whole self, you will integrate it, and it will not bother you in yourself or in others. Your work will be done with that attribute. You will be in a state of harmony, until the next trigger presents yet another opportunity for you to further know yourself by integrating one more part.

Tracy despised bullies. She was convinced they victimized her, yet it was actually her judgment of bullies that kept interfering in her life. Her husband's work environment was filled with people who bullied, and she couldn't be on committees because she always felt overpowered. There wasn't a day during which she didn't feel victimized by people whom she labeled as "obnoxious bullies." With my coaching, Tracy did the Day 11 exercise to uncover the positive essence of bullying. She agreed that she did indeed need a pinch of its positive essence—assertiveness—in her life. Things greatly improved for her: she had more choices, the undertaking of which built her self-confidence. Then we went deeper.

How Are You Doing That to Yourself?

I asked Tracy, "How are you a bully to yourself?" She burst out crying. She was relentlessly critical of and pushy with herself; nothing she did was good enough for her. In striving for self-control and perfection, she had turned into her own abuser. Her tears wouldn't stop as she realized that the bullying she had been judging others for, she was doing to herself.

How Is That Serving You?

This process of integration requires answering difficult questions. Notice any resistance you may have. Keep reading through the process and then assess when you are ready to do this work on yourself.

When Tracy surrendered to the bully within herself, her crying came to a natural end. We moved into finding out how it was serving her to keep herself so downtrodden and crushed. Most people will violently resist this concept, yet it is a fact: repeating a pattern that doesn't allow us to function at 100% means we are getting something out of it. It's that simple. Tracy resumed crying, this time softly, with a newfound compassion for herself. Bullying herself kept her safe: when she judged herself and became paralyzed with thoughts of failing, she wouldn't actually attempt anything. As long as she kept herself in a self-imposed corner, the world out there wouldn't get her, she thought. She didn't need the world out there to get her; she was doing a great job herself.

The Positive Intention of the Dark Side

Underneath every aspect we judge is the motivation for safety, for self-protection, the misguided sense that there is security in stagnation. So we perpetuate those parts of ourself we judge in others because they keep us, in a way, safe. Tracy had condemned bullies her whole life, and yet it was her own inner bully that was disempowering her. Once she embraced the paradigm that what she judged was also within her to protect her from failing, she was able to bring compassion and integration to this abusive element in herself—and in others.

Bullies don't bother Tracy anymore. She can actually feel warmth toward them, and they don't stop her from living her life. She has also consciously added a few pinches of the positive essence of bullying: she can hold her ground when people are being pushy. Integrating her inner bully tamed it, and she is no longer victimized by her negative self-judgment either. Her life is more serene and actually in her control now.

This work of integration potentially holds the most transformative benefits for you. Living in harmony with yourself and the world is worth any momentary discomforts along the way, as you push past your comfort zone into uncharted territory. (Have I said this too many times?) Experiencing compassion for yourself and others, whom you have undoubtedly judged harshly, accepting all that you are, perfect in your imperfections, is reward enough to last you your lifetime.

WORKBOOK: DAY 25

DATE: D / M / Y

Integrating Characteristics That Trigger Us

What attribute really irritates you in others? Feel your judgment as intensely as possible. Amplify it.

How does this quality translate into action? For example, bullies push and boss others around. Arrogant people treat others rudely, with no consideration. Translate the quality you have chosen into an action.

How are you doing that to yourself?

How is that serving you? What is the positive intention of this quality?

How will the integration of this quality serve you and your Big Picture?

DAY 26

RELAX INTO SUCCESS:
WHAT IF IT IS REALLY THAT EASY?

We say we want it: SUCCESS!!! In reality, we are not programmed to succeed; we are conditioned to believe it is not truly possible. Some of us might allow ourself to succeed in some domains of our life, yet to achieve success across all areas of our life is something we regard as more of a miracle (or something that happens to someone else) than a probability. We are somewhat relieved that we are not succeeding in some areas, having been programmed, per the old adage, to *beware of still waters*. We worry that if things are too easy, a big wave will rise and hit us unexpectedly, so we justify keeping ourself small with sentences like "You can't have it all." We resign ourself to live that lie, almost with relief.

When I took an improvisational stand-up comedy workshop, I learned that the number-one rule of improv is "No blocking." This is also the first rule of brainstorming. "No blocking" means that when another comic throws you an idea, you take it and go down that road. For example, if someone on stage with you says, "Let's go skiing!" and you say, "Let's go boarding instead," you are blocking. Even if you say, "We don't have any skies," or "There is no snow," you are still blocking. The correct response is to reach into your deepest core and shout with great energy, **"Yes, let's!"** enthusiastically agreeing with *any* ideas thrown at you.

In taking this workshop, I realized how we are instinctual blockers on the stage of life. Our first response is to block or modify, which actually shuts down possibilities. When we block suggestions and ideas that come our way rather than simply receive them and then assess before we actually block, we are limiting our potential for success. Accepting a suggestion doesn't mean having to follow it. It means having an open mind to receive it and think outside your comfort zone or metaphorical box, and then choosing where to go with that suggestion. It is the same with brainstorming: individually or in a group, we throw out ideas and simply follow the flow to come up with solutions outside the regular thinking process.

Opening to Potentiality

Have you noticed that when you run into someone and pay them a compliment, most people block it? If you say, "You're looking great!" they usually say, "You're looking great, too," or "So do you," or "Are you telling me I looked terrible yesterday?" How many times have *you* done that? Not receiving is a form of blocking.

When you receive a compliment, when you open yourself to recognition, you are inviting success. Receiving life in its nuances—suggestions, acknowledgements, and other seemingly fleeting contributions to us—means living in possibility, with an open mind and an open heart, trusting that people are not out to hurt us; they're doing the best they can. Always. We, too, are always doing the best we can in any given moment.

What if relaxing into success is easy? In fact, it is easy if you follow rule number one, and then move forward out of choice, trusting that any limitation is only a self-imposed prophecy. When you are open to the probability of success and retrain yourself to see it and accept it everywhere, then you can mine each event for the treasure it holds. There is no failing, only the joy of learning lessons through experience. That is success.

Failing Is the First Step to Success

Most of us have such high standards and high expectations that we spend most of our life holding back for fear of hearing the word "no" and for fear of failing. We become perpetual blockers, making few, if any, decisions, let alone powerful ones. Blockers live their lives paralyzed. They do not acknowledge that they—or those around them—are doing the best they can. Their judgment and faultfinding, as we saw on Day 25, is a reflection of their own self-evaluation. Blockers live their life in the expectation of failing, and this state of surviving is far more stressful and nerve-wracking than actually failing.

This is your chance to embrace rule number one: What if life is more than failing or succeeding? What if it is about ongoing learning and stretching to expand into a different place? In this place, everything is a success.

Living life successfully is about living life consciously, aware of how our so-called failures impact us emotionally and physically, and ultimately how that understanding propels us toward success and fulfillment.

How would it be to go through life with an attitude that shouts **"Yes, let's!"**?

WORKBOOK: Day 26

DATE: D / M / Y

Being Aware of When and How You Block

In which areas of your life do you block?

Do you block more with certain people? Who are they?

How do you block specifically? Is there a pattern in your resistance? For example, do your responses to people often include the word "but"? If someone asks you if you are open to doing something, do you say, "Yes, but...," and put a condition on it?

What do you get out of blocking? What is your payoff?

Would you be willing to embrace the **"Yes, let's!"** *attitude for a full week and consciously open your mind and heart? (You know what I want your answer to be!)*

DAY 27

ANYTHING BUT *THAT*...
SWALLOW YOUR FROG OR TOAD

Clients often ask me, "What is the one thing I have to do to be happy, to be rich, to be fulfilled?" I respond, reversing their question, "What is the one thing you have resisted all your life that would be the hardest for you to do?" I suggest that if they want to overcome any difficulties and fully embrace their life, they identify the thing they have been resisting and do it. When my clients respond with "Anything but *that*..." I point out that they are blocking and ask them to consider how much they *really* want to be happy, rich, and fulfilled.

During a seminar with well-known business coaches and authors Sam Beckford and Steve Chandler, Sam came out with a saying—"If you have to swallow a frog, it doesn't help to look at it."—that reminded me of an Italian proverb, "Swallow the toad!" which means to do something unpleasant for a higher goal. If you have blocked something for a long time, whether it is to pursue a university degree, reconcile with your parents, take a year off, or admit to parts of your personality you are not fond of, that is your frog, and it doesn't help to just look at it. Thinking about it does not help. It must be done. If you have to swallow a frog, do it at once.

Big Picture, Small Picture, Big Frog, Small Frog

In our Big Picture, doing the hardest thing first makes perfect sense: we get it out of the way, and we are buoyed by the knowledge that our life will only get easier. If we don't do the hard things first, our procrastination and the dread of having to do them will weigh us down until we do them, or worse: our unlived life is a metaphorical death.

The anticipation of how hard something is going to be looms over our head and detracts from being in the present moment. Doing that something is a whole lot easier and more fulfilling than dreading it and pretending it doesn't bother us. Pretending always drains us of energy in the long run. In today's exercise, you will identify the frog, the thing you've been resisting, the completion of which will propel you toward a full, rich, meaningful life—and just do it.

In the Small Picture of our daily life—the practical goals that compose our Big Picture—it's very much the same. If we do the hard things first, our day will be lighter afterward, and we will be free from anxiety. I've created a new proverb for you to apply to your everyday life: "If you have to swallow a few frogs, swallow the biggest one first, and do it at once."

Stretch the Metaphor

Sometimes the frog you don't want to acknowledge is more like a pink elephant that walks in front of you, your constant companion wherever you go. Everybody else has an opinion about what you need to do to work with this elephant and unleash your power, though no one says anything, pretending, like you, that the elephant doesn't exist. They are possibly afraid of hurting you, yet their "politeness" is ultimately more hurtful to your fulfillment than squarely addressing the obstacle in front of you.

Once you identify your frog, you will be called to commit to an action. For me, it was getting a university degree, which I had resisted all my life, mostly in defiance of my parents' expectations. For you, it might be looking at your priorities and taking time off from work in order to balance and nurture your personal life. Or it might be finally completing whatever unfinished business you have pending. Whatever your next action is, notice your resistance in acknowledging that this commitment might involve some dramatic life changes.

Underneath all the tangled thoughts of resistance lies a fear of rejection, a fear that we may not be good enough. We are terrified to have people walk away from us because of our choices, so we choose stagnation—which is not choosing at all. In truth, our friends are far more likely to create distance because it is too painful for them to watch us sabotage ourself in denial of what is so obvious to them.

The frog is very important in mythology and folklore. As an amphibian, a creature that changes shape and transforms, it is a symbol of rebirth. In Egyptian mythology, the frog-headed goddess represents fertility, and the frog appears in Hindu creation myths. In Vedic tradition, frogs are deities, and they also hold an important role in Western mythology. In early Christian myths, the frog symbolizes resurrection and a higher stage of spiritual awareness. When you swallow your frog with the desire to shift into a Bigger you, you shift into a place of higher consciousness, of resurrection, of rebirth.

You know what your frog is, and probably everyone else does, too. Swallow it at once! I can assure you that living your Big life is worth a few slimy creatures down your throat. And if it's any consolation, the bigger the frog, the bigger the rewards.

WORKBOOK: Day 27

Date: D / M / Y

Identifying Your Frog

What is that one thing you have perpetually resisted facing? If you've been resisting multiple things, pick the biggest one.

What is the specific action being called for when you face your frog? For example, if your frog is to reconcile with your parents, the action to take might be to call them or write a heartfelt letter.

What prevents you from taking that action?

Choose now to swallow this frog. How does it feel to be taking this on and opening upto possibilities?

How will swallowing this frog move you toward your Big Picture?

Congratulations! You just stepped into the **"Yes, let's!"** *attitude. Give yourself a pat on the back and keep going.*

DAY 28

HAPPINESS:
ALL THERE IS TO KNOW

Many of us have gone on and on about wanting to find happiness, as if it is some secret elixir that will instantly transform our life and bring us fulfillment. We have been conditioned to link happiness with external reasons, material possessions, or random circumstances. We expect that one day our prince or princess will come and make it all better and perfect. Whether the Prince and Princess symbolize a person, a job, or money, it is always something outside ourself. We have been programmed to believe that happily-ever-after happens only after someone or something comes to our rescue. Passively waiting for the fairy tale to come true is a myth and a setup for disappointment.

If there is one thing you take away from this book, let it be this: *You are the sole and exclusive creator of your own happiness.* To expect something outside yourself to bring you happiness is completely unrealistic, and it's a relinquishing of power. It is far simpler and more empowering to put yourself in charge of your happiness by clarifying and aligning your values, your life purpose, your goals, and your Big Picture. This is the foundation on which your happiness rests. I guarantee that if you have these four elements in balance, you will feel happy. When you stand in harmony with yourself, in your true power, happiness does not need a reason. It is a gift you have the capability and competence to give to yourself.

Happiness is found in the present. Many of us are willing to postpone the feeling of happiness until the kids are older and the house is paid for, creating a utopian-life fantasy in our head, where all circumstances and people are exactly as we want them to be and everything is under our control. Often, pleasure is confused with happiness, hence our pursuit of material possessions and other sources of instant gratification. Pleasure is a momentary sensation, whereas happiness is enduring, as long as our actions are aligned with our values.

Give up the fairy tale; there is no magic pill that will suddenly make you happy. The only surefire way to consistently experience happiness is to live in accordance with your individualized life plan, as you've been designing and fulfilling it over the past twenty-seven days. Every chapter in this book has provided you a new tool, each a component of the larger structure, to go deeper into yourself and intentionally create happiness in your life.

Happiness doesn't preclude life's going sideways; life will get in the way, guaranteed. The beauty of living from your internally referenced system is that, when challenged, you can tap into all your tried-and-true resources to dance with adversity. Once you realize that *you* are the maker and shaper of your own happiness, you will be happy.

Use your state of happiness as a gauge to determine whether you are on course or off. A sustained feeling of happiness tells you that you are operating in integrity with your values, life purpose, goals, and Big Picture. An absence of happiness tells you that you are operating out of integrity—compromising your values, sabotaging your goals, denying your heart's desire, and the like. When you are moving toward your Big Picture, you feel happy. When you are moving away or are stuck, you feel unhappy.

WORKBOOK: DAY 28

DATE: D / M / Y

Happiness

In lieu of exercises today, review The Map to Happiness:

- *You are the sole and exclusive creator of your own happiness.*

- *Happiness doesn't need a reason.*

- *Happiness is in the present.*

- *Happiness is when you are in harmony with yourself.*

- *Identify and align your values, your goals, your life purpose, your Big Picture.*

- *Create a structure that keeps you operating in integrity with these four elements.*

- *Even when you are happy, life can go sideways: harness your resources and dance!*

- *Use happiness as a gauge to know if you are on track or off.*

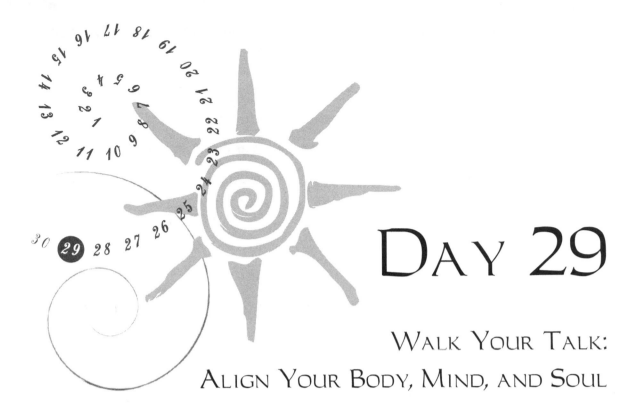

DAY 29

WALK YOUR TALK:
ALIGN YOUR BODY, MIND, AND SOUL

Our true nature as creative and resourceful human beings is to be happy and fulfilled and to have our body, mind, and soul in alignment with our heart's desire. Always. With ease and flow. Our true nature is to surrender to peace and inner joy when things go smoothly, to dance in the face of adversity, to move toward our challenges, and to appreciate and love ourself for who we are in any given moment.

As you've been moving through the chapters in this book, I am sure you've experienced many shifts in the way you perceive yourself. You've released many blocks and embraced yourself in a way you haven't done before. Notice the changes that twenty-eight days of practicing have brought you. Now imagine committing to live at your best from this moment forward. Imagine fully embracing all that you need to be and do to balance body, mind, and soul and to intentionally function at 100% capacity at all times.

In recognizing and strengthening our internal capabilities, we naturally can solve issues and deal with adversities better. We can learn to depend on our inner resources during challenging times, ever pushing our comfort zone to expand our range. When we balance and nurture the trinity—body, mind, and soul—we have all the means we need to be self-reliant.

Who Are You?

Do you walk your talk? Would you buy what you're selling from someone like you? Would you marry or date…yourself? Often we fail to ask ourself these basic questions and to honestly listen to our own answers. Some of us are in the business of wellness, yet we are out of shape. Some of us are in the business of making people laugh, though our own life is dry and humorless. Everything we do, think, eat, and breathe makes us who we are. Every little thing, even if fleeting and seemingly inconsequential, adds up to who we are in our integrity.

How we nurture our body, mind, and soul directly correlates with how we perceive life—our circumstances, other people—and, conversely, how others perceive us. We want to model in our life the attitudes and behaviors we value, the principles we believe in. We want to model congruity to our children, partners, and friends. If we want them to be patient, kind, and loving, we teach them that by being so ourself.

The Universe Within Ourself

We are our own precious universe, an interrelated system of body, mind, and soul, and we function best when these three components are working in conjunction with each other. Our body, mind, and soul will always support us to live our life at peak potential as long as we take good care of them.

How is your body? How is your mind? How is your soul? What do you want to do to support each to function at its best? Who do you need to be to look after yourself with integrity, respect, and gratitude?

Every little detail counts. Are you always late? Do you drink too much? Do you sleep enough? Do you eat junk food? Do you deprive yourself of listening to the music you love, or sacrifice some other passion because of busy-ness?

Assess who you are at your best. Assess what makes your heart sing, and purposely give yourself the things that make you happy. Now, I don't mean instant gratification. Sure, an extra cookie or glass of wine makes you feel good in the moment, skipping your workout avoids physical exertion, that designer handbag would go so well with your shoes—yet, does it support your Big Picture?

How do your habits fit you and your life in the context of your Big Picture? Please do understand that consciously making lifestyle choices fully aware of their repercussions is still better than pretending that such things don't affect you in a negative way. Have clear intention even in acknowledging that you are choosing to do some things that are not all that good for you. And be sensible: Do you really have to drink the extra glass of wine, skip your workout, and eat junk food all in the same day? Strive for balance even in your imperfect choices.

As I'd mentioned in the previous chapter, sometimes we confuse pleasure with happiness. Eating a container of ice cream might give you pleasure tonight; yet, will you be a happier person tomorrow because you have eaten it? Pleasure is often a momentary sensation; happiness comes as a result of actions aligned with values, and it's abiding. Your happiness is entirely your decision and within your control when you choose to align your body, mind, and soul. Making choices based on what makes you happy prompts you to take actions considered through the wide-angle lens of your Big Picture—actions that honor your values and beliefs, and support you in the fulfillment of your goals.

Assessing what works for you and what doesn't is essential. What is your very own formula that keeps your body, mind, and soul in perfect balance and makes you happy?

Do What You Love and It Will Be Good for You

BODY

Taking care of your body is not supposed to be a burden. If you keep skipping workouts and making excuses, your exercise routine is probably not the most suitable one for you. Every season, we are flooded with the latest fitness trends. How do you know what is right for you? The best fitness regimen is not what is fashionable; it is the one that satisfies you such that you are able to consistently practice it—and have fun doing it!

Do what you love to do. Taking care of your body is a pleasure in itself. Having your body functioning at 100% capacity is reward enough to inspire healthy exercise, healthful food choices, and sufficient rest.

MIND

Creative expression in both work and play keeps your mind bright and alive amid life's routines and practicalities. Reading a book by your favorite author, learning a foreign language, playing chess—any activity that exercises your mind—will inevitably strengthen your mental activity in all domains of your life. Do activities you enjoy, so that you stay motivated to keep your mind sharp and awake—and regularly try new ones!

Often we get so mired in what we are doing, meeting deadlines and juggling the demands of our personal and professional lives, that we lose all perspective and no longer enjoy what we are doing. If getting up from your computer screen once every hour keeps your mind from turning into mush, do it. If all it takes to keep your mind crisp is to get up and walk to a window for thirty seconds, commit to the pleasure of that interlude. Your work is not going anywhere.

SOUL

Talking about matters of the soul is a delicate task because we each have a different existential view on spirituality and the soul. Common to all of us, however, is the call to define what the soul is and what it means with respect to our true nature. Understanding and embracing your spirituality contributes to your evolution as a human being with values. How you answer the existential questions "Who am I?" and "Why am I here?" will become the filter through which you view yourself and life itself.

Every act you do, whether it is as sacred as praying or meditating, or as practical as cooking or walking or even playing sports, is an opportunity to express who you are and why you are here, and to deeply connect with your soul. Your soul will feel nurtured if your behavior is in alignment with your answers to the two existential questions. You walk your talk, true to yourself in your Big Picture.

Living in the now—in a state of being rather than of doing—in every activity you participate in, in every moment of your life, honors your spiritual essence and magnifies the experience for your body and mind.

What Comes First: The Activity or the State of Being?

Do we sing because we are happy, or are we happy because we sing? Find out what gets you going, what pumps you up, what brings you joy, what fulfills you, and choose to do those things as a habitual part of your life. Do what you love with consistency instead of as sporadic events.

Sometimes we make things so big that they are out of our reach. We fantasize about an exotic holiday or a fancy sports car that we can't afford, and we put our life on hold in the pursuit of it. Instead of living for future fulfillment, figure out what makes you happy *today*—and give it to yourself every day. It doesn't have to be extravagant or expensive. Give yourself the pleasure you find in everyday moments. If singing in the shower makes you happy, I am sure your loved ones will tolerate their momentary discomfort if it means that you are more joyful around them! Does wearing your favorite color put you in a good mood? Wear it more often: even a splash of scarf will do. If drinking a hot cup of tea fills you with contentment, buy assorted specialty teas and make yourself a cup regularly throughout the day.

Become intentional in every little detail of your life. Get to know yourself, and feed your body, mind, and soul with every wonderfully ordinary experience you can imagine that will support your Big Picture. Give yourself the gift of generating your own happiness with authenticity, integrity, and discernment.

Relevancy Check: The Impact on Your Life

For today's exercise, you will take a daring, fearless inventory of yourself and your wants, and determine the actions *you* need to take to align your body, mind, and soul. Set your intention to be the best you possible. It's quite wonderful when an action or activity crosses over into all three areas. For example, the reflective activity of meditation feeds all three areas, relaxing the body, quieting the mind, and accessing the soul. Don't limit yourself, however, to any one expression that nourishes all three areas. There are many practical activities that cross over into all three areas—dancing, walking the dog, exercising, playing golf—as well as others the combination of which feeds your whole self. Be creative: find out what works for you and what brings you closer to your ideal alignment on all three levels.

Once you have established what sustains your physical, mental, and spiritual well-being, you will assess the current conditions of your life and design a balanced plan that enables you to give yourself what you need to be happy. Negotiating with your intimate partner to find the time and/or money to do the things that fulfill you might be in order. Be true to yourself and considerate of others: create a structure that supports you yet doesn't upset the people in your life. Keep your loved ones in your Big Picture, and you may find mutual activities that are fun to do together that also support your individual well-being.

Come from the zone so that you are clear in identifying what generates good feelings in you. Be creative in designing a structure that facilitates your remembering to do the activities until they are an instinctive, habitual part of your day. Keep your focus on the rewards for yourself and others. Remind yourself that setting up a structure to practice what makes you happy is the way you create good habits—and if your habits are in alignment with your body, mind, and soul, you will inevitably function at 100%.

Dance in Harmony

When we give ourself what truly fulfills us, our integrity and authenticity harmonize us with the world around us. It's a pleasure to be around people who are genuine, and our friends, family, partner, and colleagues will reaffirm that by enjoying our company. Priceless is the contribution we give to the world when we take care of ourself from a true desire to be the best we can be.

It is an important developmental task to learn to live our life as a discerning adult who says "no" to excess that does not serve us. Instead, we say "Yes!" to what works for us in our Big Picture. When we do this, we are dancing rather than walking; we are singing rather than talking—and the most beautiful part of this harmonic movement is that the entire world sings and dances with us.

WORKBOOK: Day 29

Date: D / M / Y

Aligning Your Body, Mind, and Soul

BODY

What does your physical body need to function at 100%?

What changes do you want to make to your current regimen so that your body functions at 100%?

- Weight

  Now: Changes that you want to make:

- Eating habits

  Now: Changes that you want to make:

- Sleeping habits

  Now: Changes that you want to make:

- Exercise

  Now: Changes that you want to make:

- Other

  Now: Changes that you want to make:

MIND

What does your mind need to function at 100%?

What specific activities do you want to do to exercise your mind and keep it open and alert?

What specific thoughts make your mind function at its optimum? What thoughts make you happiest and allow you to access the zone to find creative resources?

What will you do when a negative thought arises?

List three specific thoughts that you will engage to override negative thinking.

How do you feel when you do this?

SOUL

What does your soul need to function at 100%?

A walk in the forest, having a cup of tea alone, meditating, yoga, dancing, listening to your favorite music, praying, chanting, bird watching—any of these may be what connects you with your soul, your spiritual essence. What activities bring you closer to yourself, fill your heart and soul with joy, and give you pure fulfillment?

How do you want to feel when you connect with your soul?

Designing a Structure

Make a schedule of the daily, weekly, and monthly actions and activities that you have determined will align your body, mind, and soul. Record them in your day planner or on Post-it notes to stick on a mirror or door—whatever works for you.

DAY 30

THE NEW YOU:
EXULT AND EMBRACE THE REAL YOU

The people I coach know that I rarely talk about myself in my practice, unless I am specifically asked my personal opinion, in which case I gladly take off my coach's hat and share my experience. I am thrilled to say that my work is based on my life journey: I have experienced firsthand all my observations, writings, exercises, and suggestions. My clients are the second biggest source for fine-tuning my writings, my workshops, and my method. They tell me what has worked for them, and this book is a compilation of those exercises that produced powerful results.

In life, there is no one magic step that fixes it all. That would make it a tactic, and tactics take you only so far. A successful life is defined by a multilayered, individualized formula that can support *you* to move forward with consistency and integrity. That is a strategy, and it takes you into account, above and beyond anyone or anything else, with everyone and everything that is relevant to you. The tools you have learned and practiced in this book are all steps to support you in creating your well-balanced, yet flexible, formula for success. Deepen your formula by reading my other books, receiving my coaching, participating in my telephone workshops—everything I design is for you to succeed. When you are in the driver's seat of your life, moving forward out of choice rather than reaction, you can choose your actions coming from your heart's desire and be in charge of your own destiny. And when life gets in the way, you will be ready to dance in the moment.

Now that you have learned how to become the powerful creator of your own happiness, you will predictably want those around you to change so that they, too, can be happy, successful, and fulfilled. Modeling is always the most effective and best received strategy. You want your friends to be happy? You be happy. You want your children to do well in their lives? You do well in your life. You want your partner to listen more to you? You listen more to your partner.

Exulting and embracing the real you is an attitude that takes a fearless outlook on the self and a powerful surrender to all that you are—in a word, courage. Live your life with intention, drop your defenses, and acknowledge your strengths and your shortcomings, not from a place of judgment—rather, from simply knowing who you are.

You are doing this work not just for yourself. You are doing it for your loved ones, your friends, your community, the world—and I thank you from the bottom of my thump-thump-thumping heart for sticking your neck out and embracing your journey. I thank you for sharing this part of your journey with me, and I invite you to do one more thing: restart this book tomorrow. You may download from my website, www.lunacoaching.com, the work pages, formatted in Microsoft Word, so that you can copy them to your computer and do this thirty-day process again and again, and with each big project you launch. You will not only master very practical tools for a better life, you will also deepen your self-understanding as your grow and change.

You will always be happier and more fulfilled—and can one ever be too happy and too fulfilled?

At the beginning of every passage through the book, ask yourself whether you want to pursue the same heart's desire and goals of your initial process, or a new set, and listen to your own voice. Hear it clearer and clearer every time you do this work, so that you can really, *really* get what you want. You best serve the world when you play Big.

With appreciation and respect,

Summary of 30 Days to a New You

❧ DAY 1 ❧
Define your heart's desire: What excites you and gives you passion?

❧ DAY 7 ❧
Assess your parachute and practice jumping.

❧ DAY 8 ❧
Define the steps you have to take to reach your goals.

❧ DAY 2 ❧
Make a list of goals that will support you to live a life of passion and excitement.

❧ DAY 6 ❧
Reconnect with curiosity in its purest form: ask questions without knowing the answers (and you will reconnect with the world).

❧ DAY 9 ❧
Become the Observer: Embrace the "lighthouse" perspective and look at your life with a grand-angle lens. Your Big Picture includes you, your goals, and your journey – with equal importance.

❧ DAY 3 ❧
Reconnect with your Big vision and your purpose: Who are you and what are you supposed to do in this lifetime?

❧ DAY 5 ❧
Update who you are in the present, and let go of the stories that hold you back. (Live your life!)

❧ DAY 4 ❧
Create the atmosphere that is most conducive for your reaching your goals by putting in place the parameters, actions, and thoughts consonant with your heart's desire.

❧ DAY 10 ❧
What has worked for you in the past? What hasn't? Become curious and clean house.

Summary of 30 Days to a New You

~ DAY 11 ~
A good minestrone is the one with the most flavors. Imagine yourself as the ultimate soup, and add pinches of all qualities, especially the ones that irritate you most.

~ DAY 12 ~
Conduct a self-assessment with discernment, not judgment.

~ DAY 13 ~
Watch your language: kick the word but in the butt, and when you hear yourself saying any of these words – need to, should, shouldn't – say instead that you either want to or you don't want to.

~ DAY 17 ~
What attitude would serve you best? The one that supports you or the one that holds you back? You have a choice: You get to hold only one thought at a time. (Hopefully this is an easy choice at this point!)

~ DAY 16 ~
Speak your secret out loud.

~ DAY 15 ~
What is a secret you are terribly ashamed of? Admit it to yourself.

~ DAY 14 ~
Ignite your own fire by reconnecting to your Original Spark.

~ DAY 18 ~
Define your bottom line. Focus on what you really want, and kiss goodbye what you don't want – gone... bye-bye.

~ DAY 19 ~
Balance your rational thinking with your intuitive thinking, and you will integrate the intuitive wisdom of the body with the practical perception of the mind.

~ DAY 20 ~
Empower your relationships and deep connections by doing one thing at a time. Do less to achieve more.

Summary of 30 Days to a New You

❧ DAY 21 ❧
Notice who you are being while you are doing.

❧ DAY 22 ❧
Laugh, sing, and dance to tap into your place of abundant creativity and resources. Enter the zone!

❧ DAY 23 ❧
Identify and breathe the oxygen you need to then be able to support others.

❧ DAY 26 ❧
Yes, Let's!
Relax into success. (It is really easy!)

❧ DAY 24 ❧
Smell the roses and your own scent.

❧ DAY 25 ❧
Harmonize with all parts of yourself to be in tune with the whole wide world.

❧ DAY 29 ❧
Walk your talk: Would you buy what you're selling? Would you date... yourself? Align mind, body, and soul: You are what you think, what you eat, what you drink, what you feel.

❧ DAY 27 ❧
Do the hardest thing first: Yum, swallow that frog (you can add garlic!).

❧ DAY 28 ❧
You are the sole and exclusive creator of your own happiness.

❧ DAY 30 ❧
You best serve the world when you are playing Big!

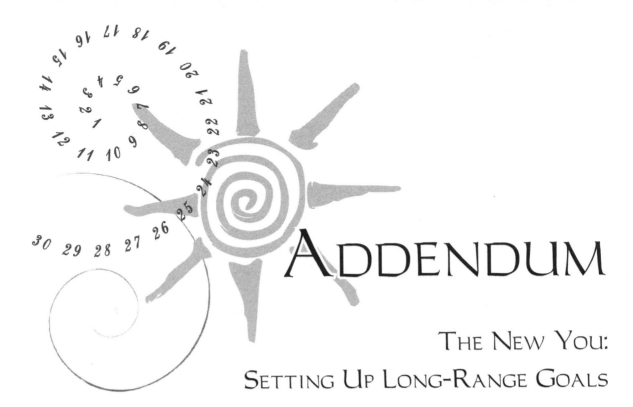

ADDENDUM

THE NEW YOU:
SETTING UP LONG-RANGE GOALS

Break each goal down into smaller time increments:

- If it's a 10-year goal, for example, break it down into 10 steps = 1 step/year; pick the same time each year to assess your results (including how you feel and if you are in synch with your heart's desire).
- If it's a year-long range, then break it down into trimesters.

By month/year_____ my goal is to _____.

Steps: Completion Date:

By month/year_____ my goal is to_____.

Steps: Completion Date:

By month/year_____ my goal is to_____.

Steps: Completion Date:

By month/year_____ my goal is to_____.

Steps: Completion Date:

By month/year_____ my goal is to_____.

Steps: Completion Date:

What's Next 4 you?

Monica is committed to continually developing programs and products for people who are interested in creating long-lasting changes in their lives. To experience optimal results, it can be extremely valuable to come from different angles and perspectives, so Monica has developed an approach that is multilayered, allowing you to devise a formula that is just right for you. Books, a CD, workshops, coaching sessions (individual or group coaching)—all of Monica's products and programs are designed to complement each other to provide long-term results. Used individually or in combination, these are valuable tools that can help you define and articulate your personal values, establish goals, and maintain the flexibility to stay connected to the lifelong process of growth

Monica's two previous books, *Being in the Present: How to Create the Blueprint of Your Life* and *Outsmart Stress! Understanding the Dynamics behind Stress*, as well as her CD, *Being in the Present: What Exists Between a Second Ago and a Second From Now?*, are perfect companions to *30 Days to a New You*.

Monica's books are designed to be read multiple times, helping you stay connected with your unique life's journey. Every time you read the books or listen to the CD, you will reach an even deeper understanding of yourself, which can lead to more fulfillment in your personal life as well as in your business life—to yield a multifaceted life filled with abundance.

With a deep personal belief and practical, worldly experience that demonstrates the incredible success people can achieve through coaching, Monica is passionate about guiding her clients down a path of self-discovery that leads to increased confidence and life balance. The key, most innovative element in her CD, her books, and her coaching sessions is that they don't give advice; they support people in finding their own answers to their questions. With these tools, you can create your own life, supported by the values that are important to you. It's *your* life, and *you* are the expert. Let Monica be your guide to achieving a life of harmonious intention.

Monica invites you to visit www.lunacoaching.com and click on "Products" and "Coaching," respectively, for the current product list and program schedules.

Books by Monica Magnetti:

30 Days to a New You: Get What You Want Through Authentic Change
ISBN 978-1-934759-07-3

Both a manual and a workbook, *30 Days to a New You* provides practical techniques and support so you can redefine yourself into someone capable of getting what you want, and capable of living life fully, with deliberate intention. Using a simple, systematic method, this book shows you how to use your infinite, individual power to connect with your real self and your powerful individual vision, while it leads you through the steps to put your new knowledge and skills into practice.

Being in the Present: How to Create the Blueprint of Your Life
ISBN 978-0-9782612-0-7 (Order at www.lunacoaching.com.)

Become the architect of your own life with this breakthrough journal and workbook, which provides a flexible, step-by-step method for writing your own life's instruction manual. Balance all aspects of life so you can achieve success and happiness. Learn how to become the leader of your own life as you are guided on a process of discovery toward living in harmony with your true purpose.

Being in the Present: What Exists Between a Second Ago and a Second From Now?
(CD-ROM, Order at www.lunacoaching.com.)

This guided meditation is designed to place you in the perfect frame of mind to achieve clarity. Use this audio CD to focus on what exists between a second ago and a second from now. Once you do, you'll be equipped to make important life decisions more quickly, with more clarity.

Outsmart Stress! Understanding the Dynamics behind Stress
ISBN 978-0-9782612-4-5 (Order at www.lunacoaching.com.)

Reclaim your peace of mind by exploring the dynamics that cause stress, and learn how to create unique ways to keep stress from controlling you. *Outsmart Stress* supports you as you learn to center yourself in the present, where you can make the correct assessment of your unique situation. Above all, it will assist you in your own personal journey, with exercises and tools designed to be flexible to fit your needs.

Coaching Programs by Monica Magnetti:

Monica offers a selection of seminars and workshops, as well as individual coaching, to support you in every way as you design your formula for success.

All of Monica's workshops and seminars are custom-designed for the participants and their needs. Monica also offers her workshops and seminars to corporations and institutions, and tailors each one to meet their unique needs.

The most popular programs from Luna Coaching, Monica's company, include:

Being in the Present: How to Create the Blueprint of Your Life

Map your unique journey in detail in this workshop, which is designed to support you after you've worked through the book of the same title. Continue to collect the benefits of being the writer of your own life's instruction manual. Stay on track by fine-tuning the ultimate blueprint of your life's journey. Join Monica for more group play and writing exercises, which will help you discover more methods for building an individual plan you can implement to guide your journey to personal success.

Become the architect of your own life.

30 Days to a New You: Get What You Want Through Authentic Change

Commit to reach your personal and professional goals while living a fulfilled and balanced life. Take proactive steps now to create the life you envision for yourself. In this workshop, you will investigate and upgrade your operating system and learn tools to get what you want in your personal and professional lives. Join Monica in this effective coaching workshop to learn methods of proactively mapping your route to success.

Get what you want and live your life now.

Outsmart Stress! Group Workshop

Learn what it takes to outsmart stress. This workshop reviews in detail the powerful dynamics that cause stress and teaches you how to regain individual control and peace of mind. Define your own successful individual formula for avoiding stress. Learn how to implement and practice stepping into optimal wellness by being prepared. Join Monica and discover how good life is when stress is outsmarted.

Reclaim your peace of mind.

Recommended Reading

Being in the Present: How to Create the Blueprint of Your Life by Monica Magnetti

Outsmart Stress! Understanding the Dynamics behind Stress by Monica Magnetti

9 Lies That Are Holding Your Business Back: And the Truth That Will Set It Free by Steve Chandler and Sam Beckford

100 Ways to Motivate Yourself: Change Your Life Forever by Steve Chandler

100 Ways to Create Wealth (100 Ways) by Steve Chandler and Sam Beckford

The Small Business Millionaire: A Novel of Heartbreak and Prosperity by Steve Chandler and Sam Beckford

Loving What Is: Four Questions That Can Change Your Life by Byron Katie

I Need Your Love—Is That True? How to Stop Seeking Love, Approval, and Appreciation and Start Finding Them Instead by Byron Katie

A Return to Love: Reflections on the Principles of a Course in Miracles by Marianne Williamson

The Dark Side of the Light Chasers by Debbie Ford

The Secret of the Shadow: The Power of Owning Your Story by Debbie Ford

When the Body Says No: The Cost of Hidden Stress by Gabor Maté

The Complete Doctor's Stress Solution: Understanding, Treating, and Preventing Stress-Related Illnesses by Penny Kendall-Reed and Stephen Reed

Blogwild! A Guide for Small Business Blogging by Andy Wibbels

ABOUT MONICA MAGNETTI

Monica Magnetti has changed hundreds of lives in the last four years as a Vancouver-based certified professional life/business and wellness coach. With her guidance, both men and women have taken control of their own life and transformed their chance at happiness and success. Monica's mission is to support individuals in finding their own tools and a formula for living life to the fullest, with enthusiasm, abundance, and prosperity. She says, "Life is about optimal wellness, vibrant force, vital energy, and alive power." Monica desires that everyone be able to embody these essences with an open heart and enthusiasm so they can be their own leader in the exciting adventure of life.

In her coaching practice, Monica uses powerful questions, discussion, exercises, journaling, and other self-discovery techniques with individuals, privately and in groups. She supports her clients as they strive to identify their life's true purpose and learn to balance their personal, intellectual, family, business, financial, and leisure lives to achieve the most satisfaction.

Monica's keen and focused entrepreneurial skills have allowed her to develop many methods to support others. Her enhanced ability to see the "big picture" in detailed steps enables her to coach her clients to reach their goals by using similar skills. For example, she thinks in PowerPoint® and has refined list-making to an art. Whether clients want to make more money, publish books, find a better job, or create the perfect balance in their life between being and doing, Monica's unique coaching approach makes it happen. *30 Days to a New You* is the ultimate list for anyone who wants to accomplish anything.

Monica is intensely creative and attuned to beauty. She marvels at everything in nature and sees strong connections between all layers of the world, including humankind. Employing her heightened senses and curiosity, Monica is a successful photographer, multimedia artist, opera lyricist, and storyteller.

Monica earned her certification with The Coaches Training Institute of California (recognized by the International Coach Federation) in 2005 and has completed her specialization in individual and group coaching. She received a BFA in creative writing in 2004 from the University of British Columbia. Monica is presently writing one more book scheduled for publication in 2008, as well as developing other products to enhance her coaching practice.

To learn more about Monica and read her articles, please visit www.lunacoaching.com.

More Empowering Books For Your Success!

Call in your order for fast service and quantity discounts!
(541) 347- 9882

OR order on-line at www.rdrpublishers.com using PayPal.
OR order by mail: Make a copy of this form; enclose payment information:
Robert D. Reed Publishers
1380 Face Rock Drive, Bandon, OR 97411
Note: Shipping is $3.50 1st book + $1 for each additional book.

Send indicated books to:

Name: _____

Address: _____

City: _____ State: _____ Zip: _____

Phone: _____ Fax: _____ Cell: _____

E-Mail: _____

Payment by check ☐ or credit card ☐ (All major credit cards are accepted)

Name on card: _____

Card Number: _____

Exp. Date: _____ Last 3-Digit number on back of card: _____

	Qty
30 Days to a New You	
by Monica Magnetti $19.95	_____
100 Ways to Create Wealth	
by Steve Chandler and Sam Beckford $24.95	_____
Ten Commitments to Your Success	
by Steve Chandler $11.95	_____
The Chic Entrepreneur	
by Elizabeth Gordon $14.95	_____
Who's Hiding in Your Address Book	
by Mary Kurek $12.95	_____
How Bad Do You Really Want It	
by Tom Massey $19.95	_____
The Secret of Transitions	
by Jim Manton $14.95	_____
All You Need is HART!	
by Helene Rothschild $14.95	_____

Quantity: _____ Amount: _____

+ Postage: _____

Total Amount: _____

Visit www.rdrpublishers.com for more great titles!